SPANISH BA~~LLADS~~

EDITED WITH INTRODUCTION,
NOTES & BIBLIOGRAPHY
BY COLIN SMITH

SECOND EDITION

PUBLISHED BY BRISTOL CLASSICAL PRESS
GENERAL EDITOR: JOHN H. BETTS
SPANISH TEXTS SERIES EDITOR: PAUL LEWIS-SMITH

Cover illustration: Woodcut reproduced by permission of the Syndics of
Cambridge University Library from a chap-book of 1515-19 via F.J. Norton &
Edward M. Wilson *Two Spanish Verse Chap-books*, Cambridge: CUP, 1969, p.73

First published in 1996 by
Bristol Classical Press
an imprint of
Gerald Duckworth & Co. Ltd
The Old Piano Factory
48 Hoxton Square, London N1 6PB

A catalogue record for this book is available
from the British Library

ISBN 1-85399-445-6

Available in USA and Canada from:
Focus Information Group
PO Box 369
Newburyport
MA 01950

Printed in Great Britain by
Booksprint, Bristol

CONTENTS

PREFACE TO THE NEW EDITION

The first edition of this book was published by Pergamon Press of Oxford in 1964. It had a modest but steady success with school and university students and general readers in Britain and the U.S., and further afield, and went out of print in 1986. I was delighted when Bristol Classical Press made the invitation to republish the work, since (as remarked in the 1964 preface) 'the ballads are fine poetry, and the *Romancero* is a compendium of fact and fancy that will teach students of Spain a great deal about the country, her history, and her people.' They were one of the texts which at a very early stage locked me into love for the language and its poetry.

In 1964 it seemed necessary to offer in the introductory materials and in the notes an account of the work of Don Ramón Menéndez Pidal on the ballads (among so much else that he achieved in a long lifetime of mighty endeavours). Much of this remains fundamental and should be of interest not only to students of Spanish but to those of English and American literature also, and much more widely than that. However, in the past thirty years there has been published a massive amount of research on all aspects of the ballads, and some of Don Ramón's ideas now need modification. Some sections of the Introduction to this book have accordingly been rewritten, and the bibliographical references have naturally been revised and much extended.

In 1991 Roger Wright published his *Spanish Ballads* in the *Critical Guides* series, taking my Pergamon book (still in print when he had more or less finished his work) as the basis of his commentary and discussion. It is to be hoped that this excellent guide will accompany my reissued texts in the hands of many readers. Since this will often be the case, I have resolved not to try to incorporate Wright's comments into my own, and not to use my notes to each text or group of texts in order to answer him on points over which we may (rarely) disagree.

Acknowledgements for help on certain points in the original edition were made to Audrey Peet, Keith Goddard, and Ben Isserlin. My thanks are due to correspondents and especially to the reviewers of the original edition, who were kindly, perceptive, and generous in their welcome for the book. I have learned much from them. One knowledgeable review was that by my friend (as he later became) Sam Armistead now of the University of California at Davis. Among Britons and Americans, he is by far the most expert in the history and analysis of the *Romancero*, particularly in the modern oral tradition which is represented in this book only by allusion, and it seems appropriate to dedicate the volume to him.

June 1995   Colin Smith

iv

ABBREVIATIONS

Canc. de rom.	*Cancionero de romances*
Gibson	J.Y. Gibson, *The Cid Ballads, and other Poems and Translations from Spanish and German*, 2nd edn (London: Kegan Paul etc., 1898)
Le Strange	*Spanish Ballads*, edited by G. Le Strange (Cambridge: CUP, 1920)
Lockhart	*Ancient Spanish Ballads, Historical and Romantic*, translated, with notes, by J.G. Lockhart; I have used the editions of 1856 and 1890 (London: John Murray)
Prim.	*Primavera y flor de romances* (of Wolf & Hofmann, 1856), reprinted with additions by M. Menéndez y Pelayo as vols VIII & IX of *Antología de poetas líricos castellanos* (Madrid: Biblioteca Clásica, 1899); reprinted as vols XXIV and XXV of *Edición nacional de las obras completas de...* (Santander: CSIC, 1945)
Rom. hisp.	R. Menéndez Pidal, *Romancero hispánico (hispano-portugués, americano y sefardí)*, 2 vols (Madrid: Espasa-Calpe, 1953)
Rom. trad.	R. Menéndez Pidal and others, *Romancero tradicional de las lenguas hispánicas (español-portugués-catalán-sefardí)*, 12 vols (Madrid: Seminario Menéndez Pidal & Gredos, 1957-85)
Tratado	M. Menéndez y Pelayo, *Tratado de los romances viejos*, in *Antología de poetas líricos castellanos* (Madrid: Biblioteca Clásica), vols XI (1903) and XII (1906); reprinted as vols XXII and XXIII of the *Edición nacional de las obras completas de...* (Santander: CSIC, 1944)
Wright, *CG*	R. Wright, *Spanish Ballads*, No. 52 in the series *Critical Guides to Spanish Texts* (London: Grant & Cutler and Tamesis Books, 1991)
Wright, translation	R. Wright, *Spanish Ballads with English Verse Translations* (Warminster: Aris & Phillips, 1987)

INTRODUCTION

1. WHAT IS A BALLAD?

Attempts to define the ballad will meet with no greater success than the attempt to define the novel. Rather than a neatly delimited genre, ballads are a whole type and tradition of literature, touching the lyric and the sentimental folksong at one extreme, and epic at the other. They have strong connections with popular legend and folklore, and their themes are often international. Their origins and development are imperfectly known and the subject of much debate. However, if we confine our attention to the more ancient and traditional ballads of Spain and Britain, a few generalisations can be risked:

(a) The ballad, although here presented as a poetic text, is really a song, and the tune may be as traditional as the words.

(b) The ballad is essentially anonymous. Although it must at its origin have had a single author, usually a poet or minstrel whose profession it was to create (or adapt) and perform such works, his name was not attached to his creation because his rôle was very different from, for example, that of Shakespeare in creating a sonnet. The ballad, after its composition by the individual author, passed into the popular domain and became universal property. Anyone could sing it, trying to recall the received text accurately (out of respect for tradition), but also anyone with the right instinct could alter the text in a major or minor way. If a new version had an obvious superiority it might become the standard one over a wide area, but always many minor variants could coexist. It follows that the ballad of tradition can hardly ever be said to have a single or a best text like a Shakespeare sonnet. Moreover, it is impossible by studying all known versions – and there may be hundreds – to reconstruct exactly the hypothetical original. The ballad is essentially fluid, 'poesía que vive en variantes' (Menéndez Pidal), though some critics prefer to insist on the relative fidelity of memory to a respected text and to emphasise the influence of written and printed texts. (For further details, see 3b below. The best analogy for modern societies bereft of ballads is with an elaborate funny story told by a TV or radio comedian one evening and repeated next day in thousands of trains, offices, and bars in perhaps hundreds of different versions, some embroidered, some shortened, each of which may produce new versions as it is propagated. But one could always check these against a recording of the original broadcast.)

(c) The older ballad had, in fact or potentially, a very long life. It was part of an oral heritage, now surviving in a pure form only in the more remote parts of Europe and America, and destined no doubt to vanish there before the advance of mass communications, entertainments, and education, and of urban-industrial civilisation. The printing-press as such did not kill the traditional ballad[1] – indeed in 16th-century Spain the press seems to have given it a considerable impetus – but it is undeniable that in recent times the ballads survived best in semi-literate societies, particularly peasant communities, and in communities which while urban and literate were marginalised and inward-looking, such as those of the Sephardim. New types of ballad have of course sprung up in our century, having themes and forms more suited to our times and even peculiar to our urban-industrial culture: one thinks of the patriotic ballads of the Irish troubles of 1916-22, of the American ballads about low life and crimes of passion, and most of all, of Caribbean calypsos. Although some of these new ballads have great interest and appeal, they are radically different from the older poems in theme and in sentiment, and are generally inferior to them as poetry. One suspects that if they are to survive it will be as semi-popular forms needing the support of the book and the electronic recording, and that they will be better-known among student groups than to the population at large. The older ballad was fundamentally oral: the singer produced it from memory, performed it orally, and by purely oral means it was passed from singer to singer and down the generations. Ballad poetry, more than any other poetry, needs (in the absence of the music) to be read aloud if it is to be savoured to the full.

(d) The ballad is largely narrative in structure and tone, though it may have long passages in direct speech (particularly dialogue) and intensely dramatic moments. The narrator only rarely intrudes himself upon the scene, but acts in an objective, impersonal way, like the eye of the camera; but like the camera, he often selects and highlights a significant detail. Facts are stated and left to work by themselves upon the hearer's imagination. There is often considerable emotional content, but the emotion is implied, not described and insisted upon at length or in a lyrical way. In the ballad of the Prisoner, for example (No. 69), we have begun to feel intensely what it is like to be imprisoned several lines before the speaker describes his own wretchedness (*triste, cuitado*). Many ballads are about love-affairs and husband-wife situations, but they are not lovesongs. (Here one notes the difference between the ballad on the one hand, and the courtly lyric, the popular lyric, and the folksong on the other.)

(e) The ballad does not moralise. Treachery, cowardice, and sexual misdemeanour produce their own tragedies, the point of which is implicit and does not need to be preached. (Here one notes the contrast between the ballad and that didactic verse so typical of the later Middle Ages.)

(f) The ballad is dignified and staid. Its ending is often tragic; if 'happy', of that species of happiness which comes as a gasp of relief rather than as merriment. Humour is rarely present in the ballads (the Scottish *Get up and bar the door* is quite exceptional), though there are often ironical notes. Nationalistic themes are almost excluded; patriotism is implied rather than stated brazenly, and a noble sympathy for one's defeated enemies is a typical feature. The theme of the ballad is not national affairs but a small human drama, whether of a military or supernatural or amorous kind. (Here one notes how the ballad differs from epic.)

(g) The language of the ballads is rapid, plain, and unencumbered by metaphor, personification, symbol, etc., which more sophisticated poets use; but the ballads have their own simple rhetoric, their very distinctive manner (see 4b below), and simple words may carry a strong charge of suggestion. The language convinces. It is forceful without being unduly sentimental or insistent. Euphemism is not common, and there is a certain frankness about sexual matters. Nouns and verbs (dynamic words, of action) predominate over adjectives (static words). Archaism in moderation is permissible, even necessary, a conventional and much-loved element which accompanies subjects which were (by the 16th century in Spain, for example) themselves often archaic.

(h) The appeal of the ballad should be high among all sorts and conditions of people at all adult ages, and among children too, although these may not understand all the implications. It should not be possible for an adult, literate or not, to say 'I do not understand it'; and all should be capable of responding to its simple, universal emotions. The ballad is for all, and reminds us that the common denominator of taste need not be a low one. The ballad manner is deceptively simple but quite inimitable. Modern imitations of traditional ballads by erudite poets in English (e.g. Scott, Wordsworth, Coleridge, Tennyson) and German (e.g. Uhland, Bürger, Goethe, Schiller) betray themselves by their sophisticated thought and their untypical language. (On Spanish imitations, see 2 below.) This is not, of course, to deny the excellence of the influence which the ancient ballads had upon those modern writers who had studied them: Coleridge in *The Ancient Mariner* may, for example, have learned much from their directness, their rapid narration, and their power of understatement.

2. EUROPEAN BALLADRY AND THE SPANISH *ROMANCERO*

Ballads are known from most countries in Europe, and have been spread by colonisation to North and South America, and have been taken by refugees and exiles from Iberia to N. Africa and the Near East. Within Europe, we must not suppose that all the ballads originated at the same time and in the same way. In some countries (certainly in W. Europe) the ballad was preceded in popular esteem by the lyric song and the epic, though for Spain a greater antiquity has recently been argued for them by Wright (1985-86). Most scholars hold that the first ballads can hardly be earlier than the 14th century, and the period of their greatest popularity in Spain was from the late 15th to the end of the 17th century (in Britain, 16th to 18th). Many of the early ballads in a number of countries are of the semi-epic kind, drawn either from the epic legends or based upon new events and persons. These existed in Spain, Britain, Germany, and Scandinavia. With these there grew up ballads which often used the forms of the semi-epic poems or of the early lyric, but which were concerned with domestic situations, supernatural legends, folk-motifs. In some countries, notably France and Italy, the second type of ballad much predominates, the great medieval epics of France (*chansons de geste*) having left no descendants in French in the form of traditional verse. The themes of both kinds of ballad frequently migrated from one language or country to another. Many of the themes in Spain are drawn from French epics and folk-legends, and some Spanish themes have become popular in N. Italy. Close links exist between some Scandinavian and Scottish ballads.

The Spanish ballads – the *romances*, collectively the *Romancero* – have several features which set them apart from those of the rest of Europe. They have an absolute unity of form, in contrast to the variety of forms used in other countries. An important section of them has close connections with the medieval epic, some being demonstrably reworked fragments of epics, others being developments from epic scenes or from prose chronicle versions of the same. The Spanish ballads are numerous and extremely well preserved, either in MSS of the 15th and 16th centuries and printed texts of the 16th, or in the modern oral tradition. They have, from the late 15th century onward, enjoyed the interest of scholars and the admiration of erudite poets, and they were in Spain an integral part of that Renaissance culture which elsewhere tended to an exclusive classicism and Italianism (see 3c below). Sung by all classes – in coarse or polished forms – from peasantry to royalty, the ballads were a truly national possession at a period when elsewhere they were an unregarded part of folk-culture.

It is the exceptional length and vigour of the ballad tradition of Spain which most impresses the literary historian, together with the fact that the *Romancero* seems to form a much more significant part of the national literature than is the case with ballads in other countries. There is no easy single explanation for this. Those who wish to speculate and indulge in generalisations about national character are free to do so after reading the texts. What we can say is that the ballad had early and strong beginnings in Spain because it was used to keep so much of the national past alive and to give voice to collective aspirations, and that it endured longer than elsewhere because Spain clung so tenaciously to her past – to her social and economic detriment – in the 18th and 19th centuries. The beginnings at least are not in doubt, and were a source of pride to Ganivet in his *Idearium español*:

Mientras en las Escuelas de Europa la filosofía cristiana se desmenuzaba en discusiones estériles y a veces ridículas, en nuestro país se transformaba en guerra permanente; y como la verdad no brotaba entre las plumas y tinteros, sino entre el chocar de las armas y el hervir de la sangre, no quedó consignada en los volúmenes de una biblioteca, sino en la poesía bélica popular. Nuestra *Summa* teológica y filosófica está en nuestro *Romancero*.

This relates to the 'historical' ballads which constitute a vast repository of fact and legend (of a sober rather than an extravagant kind) about the more picturesque parts of Spanish medieval history: about the Muslim conquest of 711, the origins of Castile, the wars between the early kingdoms, *mio Cid* the national hero, and the closing stages of the struggle against the Moors. The 'novelesque' ballads are an even larger store of popular characters, situations, and beliefs or attitudes.

The traditional and semi-traditional ballads that make up the *Romancero* are, however, only a part of the ballad contribution to Spanish literature. From the 16th century to the present day, erudite poets have used the ballad form for a wide variety of purposes. Such ballads by named authors and in sophisticated style are known as *romances artísticos* – or better, says Menéndez Pidal in order to avoid a slight upon the considerable artistry of the traditional ballads, as *artificiosos* or *individuales*. Their composition by some of Spain's greatest poets is a tribute to the qualities of the form. Some of the pseudo-historical and romantic ballads of Pérez de Hita, Góngora, Lope de Vega, and Quevedo in the Golden Age still have some of the traditional manner about them, but they are richer in texture and more lyrical. In the Romantic period the ballads of the Duque de Rivas and Zorrilla are outstanding, and in the 20th century the ballads of Antonio Machado (*La tierra de Alvargonzález*) and Federico García Lorca (*Romancero gitano*) are among the finest poems in the language. Machado said of his work: 'Me pareció el romance la suprema expresión de la poesía y quise escribir un nuevo Romancero.'

There was an extraordinary outburst of ballad-writing when Republican poets at the start of the Spanish Civil War in 1936 strove to inspire the people and troops. Their ballads were declaimed in passionate tones by Radio Madrid, blared by loudspeakers from the trenches at the enemy, and dropped as leaflets from aircraft. In November 1936 many were collected into a cheap booklet (now a sought-after rarity) published by the Ministry of Education. The texts are vigorous, spirited, and were doubtless effective at the time, but are mostly not great verse:

Libre de traidores ya,
por el mar Mediterráneo
navega el 'Jaime Primero',
para el pueblo conquistado.
Los oficiales traidores
el mar se los fue tragando...

There is even a section of *Romances de moros* with mention of Abence-
rrajes (see our No. 39), and in a poem about the fight for Granada some
lines which would not disgrace a genuine *fronterizo* ballad:

Campesinos de Jaén
y Málaga, la gallarda,
jinetes en bravas yeguas
cabalgan sobre Granada...

There are poems by Alberti, Aleixandre, Altolaguirre, Bergamín,
Dieste, Hernández, Prados, and others whose names figure (for other
reasons) in the histories of literature: a most remarkable testimony to the
enduring force of the *romance*, and to its adaptability. This publication was
far from unique: the genre continued, in great quantities, to inspire resis-
tance on the Republican side, and in all six collections of Civil War ballads
are known. Some poems maintain the tradition of anonymity by being
signed simply 'Un miliciano' and the like. There do not seem to be any
Franquist ballads; it has been said that there 'the *romance* was looked down
upon as a lesser verse form suitable for ignorant people' (Hart). The same
in reverse had happened in the civil war in Castile in the mid-14th century,
when ballads were composed as propaganda by both parties, but only those
of the winning side survive (see our No. 27); presumably it eventually
became dangerous to sing the songs of the losers. On the ballads of 1936-9,
an excellent brief introduction in English is provided by Hart (1988), with
bibliography.

3. THE HISTORY OF THE SPANISH BALLADS

(a) The name *romance*

The Spanish ballad is called a *romance*, and the derivation of the name
tells us something about the genre. It comes from a Vulgar Latin adverb
romanice, 'in the vernacular tongue', which in a substantivised sense
appears in the 13th and 14th centuries as *romanz*, *romançe*, 'poem in the
vernacular', i.e. not in the Latin of the clerks. This is used in the MSS of
such diverse works as the *Poema de mio Cid*, Berceo's *Sacrificio de la
misa*, the *Libro de Apolonio*, and Juan Ruiz's *Libro de buen amor*. During
the 14th century the word seems to have been restricted to the late epics

(earlier called *cantares*), and in the 15th it was naturally applied to those ballads which were reworked fragments of epics or in some way related to them. The meaning of Santillana's remark (1449) about *romançes e cantares* is debated – see below – but Menéndez Pidal and many others take it that *romançes* there means 'ballads'. In the MS *cancioneros* of the late 15th century and in the usage of Nebrija and Encina the term is firmly established in its modern sense. *Romancero*, created on the analogy of *cancionero*, took longer to become established. The anthologies of the mid-16th century appeared under the titles *Cancionero de romances* or *Silva de romances*, but the new collections of around 1600 are called *Romancero general.*[2]

The etymological sense is clearly 'poem (par excellence) in Spanish', which we can, without forcing it, extend to 'that sort of poem which is most typical of (or most native to) the Spanish people'. Juan de Valdés had already reached the same sort of conclusion, for metrical and stylistic reasons, in his *Diálogo de la lengua* (1535):

> Y siendo assí que la gentileza del metro castellano consiste en que de tal manera sea metro que parezca prosa, y que lo que se scrive se diga como se diría en prosa, tengo por buenos muchos de los romances que stan en el *Cancionero general*; porque en ellos me contenta aquel su hilo de dezir que va continuado y llano, tanto que pienso que los llaman *romances* porque son muy castos en su romance.

(b) Origins and development

In the first edition of this book in 1964 it seemed natural enough to adopt almost unquestioningly the 'traditionalist' (later, 'neotraditionalist') theory of epic and ballad origins developed and perfected by Ramón Menéndez Pidal, which applied not only to Spanish literature but to much else in Europe. Some classic studies of the British ballad were strongly traditionalist, several (e.g. those of Gummere and Kittredge) being quoted with approval by Menéndez Pidal, although they adhered too closely still to Romantic ideas about communal composition. In some ways the flowering of 'oralist' approaches since the early 1960s served to reinforce Pidalian neotraditionalism, though 'the Master' himself expressed reservations about the application of these to medieval epic. It is probably correct to say that since 1964 research and weight of argument have greatly altered ideas about how medieval epic was created in France and Spain (and the dependence of the latter on the former in some regards), while Menéndez Pidal's views of the ballad genre have remained substantially unaffected. Of course the debate continues. Whatever the value of Spanish theories or of Hispanists' ideas about Spanish, Spanish texts demand the

attention of foreign scholars because of the unusual vigour and longevity
of her heroic and other themes and of the whole ballad tradition.

The first investigations into European balladry in the late 18th and early
19th centuries both contributed to the rise of Romanticism and were in
turn strongly coloured by Romantic ideas. The first major collection,
Thomas Percy's *Reliques of Ancient English Poetry* (1765), had an early
and powerful effect on German scholars, and it was German beliefs that
came to dominate in the 19th century. The collection of texts which there
corresponds to Percy's was that of Herder (1773, 1778), and the edifice of
theory was constructed by Herder, Schlegel, Hegel, Grimm, and others.
The German Romantics esteemed all 'popular' verse and other forms of
expression as something of special value. Not only was this 'natural' poetry
of the people (*Naturpoesie*) much earlier than that of individual, sophisti-
cated poets (*Kunstpoesie*), but it had peculiar virtues of spontaneity and
artless charm. Here the Romantics were reviving and developing ancient
ideas, already present in Plato and his followers, about the superiority of
the works of Nature over anything that human artists can produce. The
16th-century humanists included the human productions of relatively
unselfconscious people among the works of Nature, and took a deep
interest in, for example, the popular wisdom treasured up in adages and
proverbs (in this Erasmus led the way, and was followed by many Spanish
scholars). In a preface to the second edition of the *Romancero general* of
Madrid, 1604, a writer – probably Lope de Vega – invites the reader to
compare the poetry of the ballads with the learned verse of his own day,
classical in tone and already tending to *culterano* complexities:

> Si fueres aficionado a la lengua española, aquí la hallarás acre-
> centada sin asperezas, antes con apazibilidad de estilo, y tan
> mañosamente que no te ofenderá la novedad; porque como este
> género de poesía (que casi corresponde a la lyrica de los griegos
> y latinos) no lleva el cuydado de las imitaciones y adorno de los
> antiguos, tiene en ella el artificio y rigor rethórico poca parte, y
> mucha el movimiento del ingenio elevado, el cual no excluye el
> arte, sino que le excede, pues lo que la naturaleza acierta sin él
> es lo perfecto.
>
> (quoted by Menéndez Pidal, *Rom. hisp.* II, 159)

To the German Romantics this *Naturpoesie* breathed the spirit of
primitive, uncorrupted man, and in some mysterious way it embodied the
soul of the nation, being composed for *das Volk im Ganzen* (Schlegel). As
to its composition, they held that *das Volk dichtet* (Grimm), a singularly
imprecise formula which was made only a little more acceptable by the
detailed explanations attempted by students of the British ballad in the
early years of this century. Some sort of communal, collective composition

by *el pueblo poeta*, a 'choral throng' (or as a hostile critic called it, a 'tribal syndicate') was envisaged. If the individual poet was mentioned, it was only to make him the mouthpiece through which the poetry-composing collectivity expressed itself.

The German and Austrian Romantic scholars had a special interest in Spain, particularly in the national theatre and the ballads. The latter were first published in collected form in modern times by Jacob Grimm (*Silva de romances viejos*, Vienna, 1815). Other collections, studies, and translations are those of the Germans Diez (1818, 1821), Depping (1817), Pandin (1823), Wolf (1841, 1846), and Huber (1844), and of the Dutch orientalist Dozy (1849). The *Primavera y flor de romances viejos* which Wolf and Hofmann edited in 1856 contains the most attractive ballads in their best 16th-century form and has become the basis of many modern editions, particularly since Menéndez y Pelayo made it widely known in Spain as volumes VIII and IX of his *Antología de poetas líricos* (1899). The French Romantics, especially Victor Hugo, had a particular interest in the ballads, but they (like the British, discussed below) contributed much less to the process of scholarly investigation.[3]

In Spain itself the ideas of the Germans were slow to penetrate. A few of them became known by the efforts of Juan Böhl de Faber (1770-1836; father of the novelist Cecilia Böhl de Faber, 'Fernán Caballero'), a Spaniard of German stock, who numbered among his publications a *Floresta de rimas antiguas españolas* (Leipzig, 1825). He was able to give some help with texts and theories to Agustín Durán, then working on the first collections of ballads to be printed in Spain in modern times (five volumes, 1828-32; in two volumes under the title *Romancero general* with 1901 texts, volumes X (1849) and XVI (1851) of the *Biblioteca de Autores Españoles*). As for the origin of the Spanish ballads, it was held throughout most of the 19th century by most scholars that the existing texts – recognised as being of 15th and 16th-century date – descended from very ancient but similar poems now lost, which had been composed in the way outlined above. The existence of epics of the 12th-13th centuries was explained in the light of contemporary theories about the *Iliad*: it was thought that the ancient ballads – *cantilenae* – were strung together by relatively learned individuals to form the long heroic narrations.

Percy's *Reliques* had, of course, deeply affected the original work and thinking of the British Romantics, particularly Coleridge, Wordsworth, and Scott. Their belief was that the British ballads had a 'literary origin', that is, that the poems were the work of individual minstrels who in many cases abridged and adapted what Scott calls 'the ancient metrical romances'. These ideas are in some ways more acceptable than those produced in Germany, but the British Romantics never looked much beyond our own shores (in this respect) and never succeeded in establishing a solid corpus of theory, with the unfortunate result that their ideas did not weigh at all with Continental scholars.

Even so, the Romantic theories of the Continent were gradually modified during the 19th century. It was proposed, first, that the long epics in detailed narrative style in all cases preceded the short, epico-lyrical ballads, and that some of the oldest ballads are fragments or reworkings of scenes from the epics (A. Bello, 1843; M. Milá y Fontanals, 1853, 1874; E. du Méril, 1858; J. Amador de los Ríos, 1863). The contrary opinion was not easily eradicated, however, and was still sustained as late as 1914–15 by H.R. Lang. It is revived, with a different emphasis, by R. Wright in recent work to be mentioned below.

Second, the notion of *el pueblo poeta* was attacked by Milá (1853), who held – as had Scott – that the ballads must have been the work of individual poets which subsequently (being so intended) became possessions of the people at large.

Third, the separation of *Naturpoesie* and *Kunstpoesie*, and the priority and superiority of the former, were recognised as Romantic myths. Modern scholarship hardly uses the terms and, knowing the enormous variety and complex history of the Spanish ballads, admits all manner of gradations between the two. What finally killed the simple Romantic ideas was the emergence in France, towards the close of the 19th century, of the doctrine known as 'individualism'. In considering epic and ballad origins, this postulates an act of creation by an individual author not very different from an act of creation by a modern poet. It demands to *voir et toucher*, *ver y palpar*, refusing to countenance the long series of lost and hypothetical versions which traditionalists accept, and dating ballads to only a few years before the earliest surviving texts. The key works of this school are those of Tiersot (1892) and Doncieux (1904) on the French ballads, and of Bédier (1912–17, etc.) on French epic.

Menéndez Pidal's work in the field of epic and ballad, from his first major publication in 1896 until the mid-1960s (he died in 1968) dwarfs that of his Spanish predecessors. He began by modifying the ideas of Milá and Menéndez y Pelayo, and challenged by the continued opposition of the French 'individualists' eventually constructed his 'neotraditionalist' theory, a critical edifice which is as complete and detailed as these things can ever hope to be. Between his ideas and those of the Romantics there remained a certain affinity. 'Neotraditionalism' recognises the part played by the individual author in the first act of creation (this in turn being influenced by existing tradition), but insists on the part played by the people at large in the long process of evolution which has led the ballads to assume their present forms. The original act of creation is important, obviously, but of importance too is the continuous modest creativity of which each successive performer partakes as he, or in recent centuries more likely she (see below) produces a version of a respected and memorised but potentially unstable ballad text. Menéndez Pidal replaced the notion of the *pueblo poeta* by that of the *autor-legión*, that is, the host of nameless individuals each of whom has contributed a mite to the development of the ballad.

Beyond this general statement it is safest to regard each type of ballad as having distinctive origins. Something more can usefully be said, however, about the relationship of the ballads to the epics.

Menéndez Pidal's view of the matter, still accepted by very many in Spanish studies, was that as the habit of reciting or chanting the epics (*cantares de gesta* such as the *Poema de mio Cid*, the *Infantes de Lara*, the *Cerco de Zamora*) declined in the 14th and early 15th centuries, they were not simply forgotten or relegated as prose accounts to libraries as were the French *chansons de geste*. Instead they lived on transformed into ballads, which took over the metrical form and much of the special language of the epics (see 4b below). The old monotonous epic chant was replaced by more sprightly ballad tunes. Only certain limited parts of the epics were reborn as ballads: the most effective and popular scenes, dramatic moments in which much direct speech was used and lyrical notes were present or might be developed. The transformation of the epic fragment was the work of the *juglares*, professional poets and musicians, whose stock-in-trade the epics had been and who knew public taste because their livelihood depended upon it.

The epic fragment sung in isolation might at first have been somewhat formless, lacking that economy and concentration which we admire in the texts known to us later. But as a fragment it was relatively short. Whereas to memorise one of the old epics of perhaps 4000 long lines, or a whole repertoire of them, had required the special powers of the trained minstrel (similar in this to the modern actor), or his skill in improvisation, anyone could take away in his head the rough text and tune of the ballad after he had heard it performed twice. The ballad thus became the possession of the people at large. Some individuals would acquire fame as active ballad-singers, called upon to perform at social gatherings and festivities, but most people would be at least inactive *possessors* of ballads. People would remember the texts with differences. An individual might have a personal version, but be unable to reproduce it twice in precisely the same way. A family or a village might have its version, with slight variation between its component individuals; and so on. If modern investigators collect 500 versions of a ballad, no two exactly correspond. If a ballad lives in this way over a period of time it becomes *traditional*, and if it began life in the late 14th or 15th centuries it is a *romance viejo*.

This *poesía que vive en variantes* is not necessarily degenerating as it does so; far from it. The variants that cause its evolution may be 'positive' or 'negative': negative when the result of mere forgetfulness, mishearing, or downright stupidity, but positive when they result in an acknowledged improvement of the text. (The accuracy with which the partially-historical material of the parent epic is remembered is no criterion.) Positive variants can hardly be produced by just anybody; each must be the invention of a person having a poetic instinct and a moment of inspiration (*un cantor en estado de gracia poética*, in a happy phrase of E. Asensio). Some of the best ballad versions, as judged on admittedly subjective criteria, are the result of reworking by highly cultured – though still mostly anonymous – poets of the Renaissance period. Positive variants have often involved a shortening of the text, to its advantage, in producing that concision and tension which are a hallmark of the best Spanish ballads, though Menéndez Pidal's doctrine on this aspect is less firm than was once the case, as shown for example in our notes to Nos. 69 and 70. Other positive variants bring about the elimination of much of the circumstantial narrative in the parent epic (details of persons, places, journeys, lines introducing speakers, etc.) and the creation of a vaguer atmosphere of *ensueño* having great poetic appeal. Sometimes sections of a quite unrelated ballad may be transferred to another, where, if the fit is good, we have another kind of positive variant.

There are also cases in which a longer ballad has been split into component scenes, each then acquiring an independent existence. In this way *Doliente estaba, doliente* (No. 14) was split from its continuation, *Morir os queredes, padre* (No. 15): they are printed separately in the *Canc. de Rom. 'sin año'* of about 1548, but the editor of the 1550 collection knew the complete version still, and included linking lines of equal antiquity. See also Nos. 25 and 26. Such splitting may represent a final stage in the fragmentation of the original epic.

The process outlined above explains, in Menéndez Pidal's terms, the development of the epic *romances viejos*, that is, of many of those in the groups represented by Nos. 4-26 and 41-9. Many of the novelesque or fictional ballads, Nos. 56-70, are equally *romances viejos* and may have evolved in the same way, but there is far more uncertainty about the manner and date of their original composition since for them no equivalent of the epic sources can be postulated. Some of them may be more ancient than the epic ballads, having originated in diverse ways (e.g. as lyrics, as poems in full rhyme, as parallelistic poems) but being fitted into the metrical form of the *romance* when this became so dominant in the 15th century. (See, for example, Nos. 61, 66). The international analogues and widespread folkloric motifs of many of these novelesque ballads also serve to make discussion of origins difficult.

Many of Menéndez Pidal's ideas about the origins of ballads in epic can be allowed to stand, but it is necessary to add to them that some poems may be adaptations and free reworkings rather than fragments of epic, while others may derive in the 14th and 15th centuries from chronicles which had incorporated prose versions of heroic tales into their texts, just as we know happened in the second half of the 16th century on a large scale when poets used printed chronicles as inspiration for 'historical' ballads.

However, the tranquil acceptance by most of Menéndez Pidal's doctrines has been disturbed by Wright in two brief but forceful articles. He suggests that ballads – defined as octosyllabic, of very varying length, and dealing with themes known to us as typical of later surviving texts – may be very much older than hitherto thought. Ballads on the Infantes de Lara and the Cid, for example, may have preceded by many years epics on these subjects, and might have influenced poets who composed these epics, as Wright argues in detail by showing how many of the fictional or tenuously historical scenes and themes of the *Poema de mio Cid* correspond to those typical of Spanish ballad literature. This is in no way a regression to 19th-century beliefs that the epics were forged from ballads arranged into cycles and strung together.

The advantages of Wright's proposal are several. One is that it would account for odd details of a fictional or pseudo-historical kind which are not present in the epic texts we have or can to some extent reconstruct but are given by two Latin chroniclers of the 13th century (1236, 1243), in passages which have no other known source. Another is that it explains the seemingly rather sudden flowering of ballads (some of the earliest we know about) as propaganda in the Castilian civil war of the mid-14th century: the contestants would more likely have used an established and popular genre than invented a new and strange one. The present editor has supported Wright to the extent of identifying a possible early ballad about the moment of the Cid's exile (Smith, 1991-2), but retains doubts (for example, concerning epic metrics) about aspects of Wright's proposal. A speedy reaction to Wright's first article was that of Armistead (1986-7); other assessments will doubtless appear.[4]

The habit of making heroic verse out of events and people of the very recent past ('neotraditionalism' insists that this was how epic was created, but 'individualism' often denies the immediacy of links between event and poetic text) can certainly be identified in the ballads known as *noticieros* or 'news-bearing'. This kind, according to Menéndez Pidal, goes back to the early 14th century, but Wright would allow it much before that. A particular type is the *fronterizo* ballad, about events on the border between Castile and Moorish Granada, represented in our collection by Nos. 27-40. Such ballads were born as ballads only a little different from their surviving forms, and were the work of professional minstrels. Although they were early and popular enough to have become traditional, they have evolved less than the epic and novelesque poems, presumably because they were considered concise and expressive enough already. 'News-bearing' is really the least of their functions: they make good poetry out of desperate actions, loss of towns, exaggerated exoticism (of the Moors), and human tragedies.

Of a different order are the ballads called *juglarescos*, the work of sophisticated and courtly poets and minstrels of the middle and late years of the 15th century. These were popular enough as printed texts and songs in the 16th century but had then (and have since) undergone little development under oral transmission. In style they have a predominance of narrative passages, and make frequent use of distinctive formulae (see 4b below). They give a full account of an often lengthy story, and lack the brevity and tautness of the *romance viejo*. Three kinds of *romances juglarescos* can be discerned: that which is a new version of a *romance viejo* of epic origin; that which is designed to fill a gap in an epic cycle (i.e. to represent an epic episode from which no *romance viejo* had derived, examples being Nos. 11 and 22); and wholly new creations unrelated to any historical event or epic source, although having a pseudo-historical or pseudo-epic air. Of this last kind are some of the Carolingian ballads, Nos. 50-4.

(c) The ballads in the 15th century and the Golden Age

The first ballad text known is no more than a nostalgic jotting made in a notebook by a Majorcan student in Italy (see No. 66). Next one finds in the MS *Cancionero de Londres*, compiled between 1471 and 1500, three ballads attributed to the Galician *trovador* Juan Rodríguez del Padrón, who flourished about 1430-40. One of these is an already much-confused version of the famous *¡Quién hubiese tal ventura!* (No. 70). Menéndez Pidal thinks it significant that the earliest records are thus made by people on the periphery of the Spanish world. Certainly when the first references to ballads are made by writers at the centre of Castilian literary culture they are unenthusiastic. Juan de Mena in his learned *Laberinto de Fortuna* (1444) knew the poem about Ferdinand IV 'el Emplazado' (1312?) but called it peasant verse:

segund dizen rústicos desto cantando (287g)

He also refers to Álora as the *villa non poco cantada* (190c), showing that he knew the ballad here printed as No. 34. Mena's friend the Marqués de Santillana shows a similar aristocratic disdain for the ballads in his *Proemio e Carta* or preface to his works (1449), the first critical account of Spanish poetry. In his scheme of values the classical poets occupy the upper places, the Italian and Occitan the middle; below them,

Infimos son aquellos que sin ningund orden, regla nin cuento fazen estos romançes e cantares de que las gentes de baxa e servil condiçión se alegran.

The objection is both to the formlessness of the ballads and to their low social category.

This lack of esteem for the ballads was soon to be rectified, and in a most unexpected place, the Court itself. From about 1460 the ballads began to enjoy a considerable vogue and were cultivated by court poets and musicians. In 1462 it is recorded that Henry IV of Castile ordered a ballad about the Granadine war to be set to music. It is possible, indeed, that such *fronterizo* ballads had enjoyed official encouragement for some decades previously. The ballads were even more esteemed at court under the Catholic Monarchs Ferdinand and Isabel. It is not to be thought that the ballads sung at court and to noblemen were the same as those which on the lips of villagers had been despised by Mena and Santillana. It was customary for the court poets and musicians to 'gloss' them, that is, to revise the words (without destroying their essential brevity, directness, and lack of sophistication), to polish the form and compose new tunes. In these more elegant modes the ballads began to be admitted to the *cancioneros* or anthologies of the late 15th century; 38 texts figure in the *Cancionero general* which was compiled from 1490 and printed in 1511. Many of these show the taste for brief versions which lasted into the mid-16th century. Carolingian, novelesque, and frontier ballads seem to have been the most favoured in the time of the Catholic Monarchs, the frontier poems receiving a special stimulus because of their value as propaganda in the war against Granada, then (towards 1492) in its bitter final stages. The enhanced status of the ballad is evidenced by the quotations made from several of them by Antonio de Nebrija in his *Gramática castellana* of 1492, and by Juan del Encina's inclusion of the ballad – full rhyme and division into quatrains being stipulated, however – among the standard Spanish forms in his *Arte de poesía castellana* of 1496.

In the 16th and 17th centuries the ballad prospered as did much else in life and in art in that great release of creative energies we call the Renaissance and the Golden Age. Ballads of every type achieved enormous popularity among all classes: beloved of musicians, profitable to printers, esteemed by scholars, imitated eventually by the greatest poets of the age, known to all, they formed a unique national heritage. The feeling which the humanists and writers who had been brought up on the classics and on Italian literature had for the ballads was infinitely stronger than that which existed in other countries for the corresponding kinds of traditional verse, and was an altogether healthy one. The reasons for this feeling, in Platonic thought as interpreted by Renaissance scholars, are well brought out by Lope de Vega in passages adduced elsewhere (pp. xiii, xliv). It must be recognised, however, as Ian Michael reminds us (1996), that the ballads as published by collectors and scholars in all centuries from the 16th until well on in the 20th (not only in Spain) have often not been totally genuine popular artifacts but have been subjected to editorial adjustments and 'improvements' of various kinds.

In Spain the special esteem accorded to the ballads is in part attributed to that spirit of national dedication which inspired the imperial enterprises and wars in defence of the faith. Although the habit of making ballad verse out of notable contemporary events virtually ended with the fall of Granada in 1492, it was natural that a people thrilling to the news of the Gran Capitán, of Cortés, and of Don John of Austria should relive in their ballads the deeds of the Cid and other heroes. But in popular favour the Carolingian and novelesque ballads ranked with the historical, and at court and among the printers the former even had an earlier vogue than the latter, so this cannot be the whole explanation. Rather one should say that the ballads picked up from the mass (*gentes de baxa e servil condición*) were brought to perfection of text and music by a number of individuals in the late 15th century, and as such were found to be to the taste of the nation in later decades. Moreover, the means to propagate these improved versions was at hand.

Menéndez Pidal tells us that the printing-presses in the 16th century turned out more ballads than any other type of verse. The ballads were at first printed, three or four together and often with other poems, on *pliegos sueltos* (typically of four leaves, being a single sheet printed on both sides and folded twice to form a quarto gathering; or of two leaves, being a half-sheet folded once).[5] These, printed from about 1506 to 1605, sold cheaply in the streets of Spanish towns and at fairs and markets. Being unbound, they rarely survived for long and are today bibliographical treasures. The first printed collection was a *Libro en el qual se contienen cincuenta romançes con sus vilancicos y desechas* printed at Barcelona by Carles Amorós at some date between about 1525 and 1530, which survives in a unique and sadly fragmentary copy. Much more ambitious and influential was the *Cancionero de romances* printed by Martín Nucio at Antwerp in about 1548, often called the '*cancionero sin año*'. It contains 150 texts, most of them printed from *pliegos sueltos* but some garnered from the memory of Spaniards resident in the Low Countries. Nucio's book was of pocket size and intended for popular circulation rather than for library use. It was reprinted several times in Spain in 1550 and the following years, with substantial alterations to Nucio's text as editors recalled or gathered superior versions and added further poems.

The printing of the old ballads with their tunes began in 1535-6 in the music-books of Luis Milán and Luis de Narváez, and continued up to that of Francisco de Salinas in 1577. In these books, however, the ballads figure no more than occasionally among many other types of lyrics and tunes. The instrument to which the ballads were sung during most of the 16th century was the *vihuela*, having 6 or 7 strings which were plucked, but at the end of the century the modern-style guitar seems to have replaced this for the purpose.

The *pliegos sueltos* and the mid-century *cancioneros de romances* gathered in between them much of the harvest of *romances viejos* and *juglarescos*, although a few were still being collected and published (among newly-composed ballads and other verse) by Juan de Timoneda in 1573 and Ginés Pérez de Hita in 1595. This can be considered a sort of not very coherent corpus, in the sense that many Spaniards would have thought this the collective *romancero* of their times as consecrated (but not fixed) in print. However, as Armistead and others have forcefully pointed out, some respectably old ballads did escape the collectors of that time and have come to light in our century, and whatever the force of the printing-press, the ballads continued to evolve in the oral and performing tradition, so that in a proper definition the *romancero* is much larger than that represented in 16th-century printings.

Due account being taken of that, the second half of the 16th century was to be the most glorious period in the history of the *romancero* as a cultural force. Not only did the older ballads continue in full vigour and enjoy new forms of life in *Don Quixote* and the theatre, but beside them diverse kinds of *romances artificiosos* acquired a vast popularity and esteem.

One can see in Cervantes (born 1547) how profoundly the ballads took hold of the imagination of a highly cultured but not untypical Spaniard of the later Renaissance. *Don Quixote* may indeed have been inspired in a small way by a certain *Entremés de los romances* (written between 1591 and 1595) in which the language and world of the ballads affect the mind of a peasant in much the way that the books of chivalry affect Don Quixote's. The noble knight and his squire quote freely from the ballads, comparing their situations with those of ballad heroes and regarding the ballad world, like that of Amadís and company, as a perfectly real one which had only just passed away.[6] This dream-world becomes reality – Don Quixote's sort of reality – in the episode of the Cave of Montesinos (chapters 22 and 23 of Part Two), one of the most touching in the book, based on the Carolingian ballads printed here as Nos. 52 and 53.

The use of ballad themes as plots for plays began in 1579 when the Sevillian Juan de la Cueva wrote as a full-length drama *La muerte del rey don Sancho*, followed by *La libertad de España por Bernardo del Carpio* and *Los siete infantes de Lara*. That infinitely large world of events and personages which the miniature drama of the ballad-text can suggest to the imagination of the reader is transported to the stage, helped out (as was Shakespeare in his historical plays at the time) by reference to printed chronicles. Cueva was followed by several anonymous playwrights and by Lope de Vega, who had such an intense feeling both for the poetry of the ballads and for the national past. He wrote some 20 plays on ballad themes, mostly during his youth. From about 1587 the *romance* metre was used in the theatre, so that Lope and others were able to quote the original ballads and to gloss them in various ways at significant points in the action. Lope's followers did not on the whole imitate him in writing ballad-plays, but one cannot omit mention of Guillén de Castro, who among eight such works composed *Las mocedades del Cid* and *Las hazañas del Cid*, of which the former (c. 1612-15) provided Corneille with the idea and materials for his masterpiece *Le Cid* (1636).[7]

The *romance artificioso* of the later 16th century began with very feeble attempts to refurbish old historical ballads and to write new ones on material drawn from the *Crónica de España* which Ocampo had published in 1541 (held to be the original of Alfonso X, but in fact a later version of it). Of this kind are the collections published in 1550 by Alonso de Fuentes and in 1551 by Lorenzo de Sepúlveda. New ballads on historical themes were written less and less as the century advanced, although a very successful collection of old and new Cid ballads was issued in 1605 by Juan de Escobar, last printed in 1757 in its 26th edition.

From about 1580 taste was turning to new types. One finds numerous pastoral ballads which continue that lyricism and delicacy of sentiment already expressed in eclogue and novel earlier in the century. There was a great vogue for *morisco* ballads which, deriving vaguely from the *fronterizo* tradition of the 15th century, exaggerate the romantic and exotic qualities of the now defeated Moors. The outstanding work here is Ginés Pérez de Hita's *Guerras civiles de Granada* (1595), a sort of historical novel interlarded with old ballads and original poems. There are fine compositions too in this genre by Lope de Vega and Góngora (including adaptations to contemporary themes which Menéndez Pidal calls *africanos* and *de cautivos*). A host of other poets acquired temporary fame as ballad-makers, particularly when their work was collected into anthologies (mostly called *Flor de romances*) which were in turn collected together in the great *Romancero general* of 1600-5. In this the change of taste is seen to be complete, for the collection consists entirely of *romances artificiosos* and the *viejos* are excluded. Later, in the hands of Quevedo and others, the heroic and pastoral themes declined further and the ballad acquired an amusing but unworthy air as the *jácara* or verse about low life.

A useful test of the popularity of the genre is the frequency of parodies of it. Occasional examples are recorded quite early in the 16th century, but they did not become common until its later years. The *morisco* ballads of

Lope de Vega were parodied from about 1585, the Carolingian from 1582 by Góngora, himself a masterly composer of serious ballads. These parodies are witty and affectionate rather than sour. Cervantes does not make fun of the ballads in any way in *Don Quixote*; while the exaggerated posturings of the books of chivalry were fair game, his respect for the Spanish heroic past is never in question. It was not Cervantes who 'laughed Spain's chivalry away' as Byron thought, but rather the following generation in the person of Quevedo (born 1580), who was the first to parody a Spanish historical ballad. His *Pavura de los Condes de Carrión* (1606) not only pokes fun at the treacherous Counts – the original epic had done that – but makes a comic figure out of the noble Cid himself. This might not be a bad way of dating the beginning of Spain's decline from greatness.

Finally, the *romancero* was highly valued in the Golden Age by historians who, like Sancho Panza, tended uncritically to accept its statements as hard facts. The relatively recent *fronterizo* ballads were particularly useful to writers on Andalusian affairs, such as the Sevillian Gonzalo Argote de Molina in his genealogical work *Nobleza de Andalucía* (1588). He has interesting versions of a number of ballads, and provided for posterity the only known text of the ancient *Cercada tiene a Baeza* (No. 27). Argote has a section on ballads in his *Discurso sobre la poesía castellana* which he prefixed to his edition of the *Conde Lucanor* (1575). He not only shows how much he valued them for historical and linguistic reasons, but hints (though he knew nothing of the epics) at the relationship between the ballad material and the medieval chronicles such as that of Alfonso X:

> En el qual género de verso al principio se celebrauan en Castilla las hazañas y proezas antiguas de los reyes, y los trances y successos assí de la paz, como de la guerra, y los hechos notables de los Condes, Caualleros y infançones, como son testimonio los romances antiguos castellanos...

> En los quales romances hasta oy día se perpetúa la memoria de los passados, y son vna buena parte de las antiguas historias castellanas, de quien el rey don Alonso se aprouechó en su historia, y en ellas se conserua la antigüedad y propriedad de nuestra lengua.

(d) The ballads in modern times

In the later 17th century there seems to have been a decline in the popularity of the *romance artificioso* (though there were still many examples among the *pliegos* that Pepys bought in Seville in 1684), and a total loss of interest among poets and scholars in the *romances viejos*. Nor was it possible for this interest to revive in the neoclassical taste of the 18th century. The traditional ballad lived on vigorously among the populace but nothing was heard of it. The intense interest of Romantic scholars in Germany and later elsewhere was nurtured largely on ballad texts printed in the 16th century, and these formed the almost exclusive basis of the great collections made by Agustín Durán between 1828 and 1851. In fact there was an astonishing unawareness in Spain of the *estado latente* in which a rich ballad tradition was managing to survive among the country people.

It was on the periphery of the Peninsula that the modern oral tradition began to come to the attention of poets and scholars, in Portugal, where in the 1820s Almeida Garrett recalled or collected a few ballads, and in Catalonia, where Milá and others began to tap rich sources from 1853. Collections from Asturias and Galicia followed, and from Andalusia, although here the tradition was evidently very weak by the end of the 19th century. In Castile proper it seemed no ballads remained, and for a time this was accepted as fact and explained. Fittingly, it was Menéndez Pidal himself who, more or less by accident, began the recovery of the Castilian ballads in the small town of Osma in May 1900. In small amounts at first but in increasing quantities as trained collectors, musicians, and folklorists got to work, the full wealth of the tradition in all parts of the Peninsula came to light. It may be true to say that it is still not fully known, and what is left is declining rapidly under modern pressures. Much study of materials gathered in the last hundred years remains to be carried out. Outside the Peninsula interesting collections have been made in most of the countries of South and Central America, the tradition being somewhat less rich than that of Spain but possibly more archaic.

Considerable attention has been given also to the ballads which survive orally to the present day among the Sephardim, the descendants of the Jews expelled from Spain in 1492. In northern Europe, Italy, etc., these quickly lost their old Spanish language and folklore, but those who took refuge in countries of inferior culture, such as lands of the old Turkish empire and N. Africa, preserved a dialect and popular literature of enormous interest. Although there is evidence that they received some texts during the 16th century, most of the ballads known among these Jews are of pre-1492 date, and their importance can be imagined. For example, the long version of *¡Quién hubiese tal ventura!* (No. 70) is known only from a Sephardic source, and such fine ballads as *En París está doña Alda* (No. 44) and *Todas las gentes dormían* (No. 49) are today remembered only among the Jews, not in Spain. Despite terrible losses suffered by the Balkan Jews in the Second World War, and much migration from settlements elsewhere, the Sephardic tradition seems able to survive tenuously in many cities of the Middle East, in Israel itself, and even among the numerous emigrants to the New World.

One must not pretend that modern versions collected from the oral tradition in Spain, in Spanish-speaking America, in Catalan, from the Portuguese tradition in Brazil, and from the Sephardim, are all pearls of great poetry. All too often they are inferior when compared with 16th-century texts, seeming sometimes confused, rambling, full of rather childish and unwarranted additions, and sometimes spoiled by intrusive religious and moralising notes. Some authorities, such as Child and Meier, together with most of the French individualists, held that 'the people' has never at any time enhanced the texts in its possession, but only caused their degeneration. But this is a question of taste, and Armistead and Silverman (who know the modern oral tradition better than most) take a more positive view.[8] Occasionally modern versions have features of interest, preserving ancient variants of which the early printers took no heed, and sometimes, of course, the oral tradition preserves ballads which escaped the notice of those printers altogether, such as *Vengo brindado, Mariana* (No. 68). The modern oral tradition is a remarkable animal breed which thrives in a sort of unconfined laboratory and is available, unaesthetised and bothered only by tape-recorders, for analysis by very distinguished specialists whose studies (a small selection only) are listed below.

The very length of the Peninsular creative and oral tradition is extraordinary, as is its diversity. Doña Alda, *la belle Aude* in the French *Chanson de Roland* of about 1100, popular for a while in successive versions of that poem, has been dead on her native soil for perhaps six centuries, but she survives to the present day in a form amply worthy of her origins, among the expelled Jews. The magic of 'Un sueño soñé, doncellas' is not easily forgotten.

4. THE ART OF THE SPANISH BALLADS

(a) Form

The ballads undoubtedly owe some of their diffusion in time and space to the excellence of their form. There is, moreover, only the one form, not a variety as there is in the ballads of Britain and other countries (but see below). This sameness is a source of strength rather than of monotony, since it makes for easy learning and facility of creation and adaptation.

The ballad line has eight syllables, this octosyllable being the basic line of many Spanish strophic forms, and of great antiquity. The line has a fairly strong stress on its 7th syllable, and may have other subsidiary stresses earlier in the line which allow a diversity of pace and rhythm. If the line has a masculine (*agudo*) ending, that syllable counts for two, in the usual Spanish way, and carries the stress:

```
  1   2   3   4     5  6  7,8
que a / tie / rra / quie / re / lle / gar
```

The ends of the lines are not rhymed in the way that is normal in modern English, French, German, or Italian, that is, in full or consonantal rhyme, but in *assonance, in which vowels alone correspond and consonants are* disregarded. The assonance unites the ends of the even-numbered lines only, and may be a pair of vowels such as *í-o*:

Rey don Sancho, rey don Sancho,
no digas que no te av*iso*,
que de dentro de Zamora
un alevoso ha sal*ido*

or of a single stressed vowel such as *ó*:

Treinta días da de plazo,
treinta días, que más n*o*;
y el que a la postre viniese
que lo diesen por traid*or*.

In some ballads it will be observed that there is what appears to be a mixture of double-vowel and single-vowel assonance. Such a case is that of No. 44, *En París está doña Alda*, in which most of the 29 rhymes are of the single type in *á* (Roldán, acompañar, calzar, etc.) but in which a few are double, in *á-e* (gr*ande*, desh*ace*, s*angre*, Roncesv*alles*). These rhymes are really the same, and all assonances are double. Up to the end of the 16th century at least the single-vowel rhymes of such a ballad were usually read – or better, sung (by popular singers though not, it appears, by court musicians) – with the addition of an extra *-e*, Roldán-*e*, acompañar-*e*, calzar-*e*, etc., producing a poem in which all the rhymes are in double-vowel assonance, *á-e*. In the 16th century ballads were often printed with this extra *-e*; it survived in song in archaic areas such as Andalusia until the early 19th century, and survives to the present day among the Sephardim of Morocco and the Eastern Mediterranean.

Normally each ballad has only one assonance maintained throughout, but there are plenty of cases in which a ballad has two or three or even more rhyme-series. Such are Nos. 10 (*á-o, á-a, á*) and 12, and even in the very short poems Nos. 23 (26 lines) and 46 (28 lines) there are changes of rhyme. Such a change of assonance shows that the ballad is ancient, since different rhyme-series correspond to successive paragraphs of series (*laisses, tiradas*) in the original epic. The more recent ballads, such as the *fronterizos* and the new Carolingian creations of the 15th century, even if of great extent, never have more than a single rhyme. In the late 15th and during the 16th century older ballads were sometimes rewritten to reduce a variety of assonance-series to uniformity.

Assonance is so typical that it has been called 'Spanish rhyme'. It is however known in some medieval Latin verse and in the oldest French epics. The Spanish epic is written in it, as are the 'Mozarabic' lyrics and much popular-style verse in Castile, Portugal, etc. It had an astonishing revival in the mid-19th century, being used by Bécquer to rhyme a variety of strophic forms, and is much used by 20th-century poets as a compromise between the restrictions of full rhyme and the formlessness of blank verse (which is less successful in Spanish than in English).

In length the ballads vary considerably. The shortest, including *Por mayo era, por mayo* (No. 69) have only 16 lines; the longest in this book, *Medianoche era por filo* (No. 54) has 412, but another famous Carolingian ballad of Conde Dirlos extends to 1366. Different periods have had different tastes. The tendency of the ballads based on epics was, as explained above, to contract as unnecessary details were eliminated, and this tendency reached an extreme in the early 16th century with the taste for beginnings *ex abrupto* and for endings which stopped short of the dénouement, producing suspense and mystery. The *romances juglarescos* of the 15th century are often of the type called by Menéndez Pidal *romance-cuento*, more similar to ballads of other countries in that they tell a full story. New ballads of the later Golden Age, and new versions of old ballads then made, also tend to be full narrations in which everything is duly (and rather prosaically) explained, and the same is often true of versions circulating in the modern oral tradition. The average length of ballads in this book, excluding the untypical *Medianoche era por filo*, is about 50 lines.

It is of course possible to print the ballads in long lines of 16 syllables, treating each octosyllable as no more than a hemistich or half-line, and allowing the assonance to fall at the end of every line. Such a method of printing may better represent the early relationship of the ballad form to that of epic, though this is still unclear (Wright's recent equation of the two is not acceptable). Although the early 13th-century *Poema de mio Cid* – the only nearly complete epic text we have – appears so highly irregular in its versification, which probably did not have a syllabic basis at all, the tendency in what we can find or reconstruct of later epic texts was towards a greater predominance of 16-syllable lines, though still with much irregularity. The old ballads which were fragments of (or otherwise related to) epic took over and consolidated this tendency towards the line of 16 (or 8 + 8) syllables. Two factors helped to establish the ballad line as a regular double octosyllable. On the one hand courtly and learned poets who became interested in the ballad in the late 15th century naturally preferred tidiness and regularity to disorder (as Santillana implied). On the other, the full and often lively tune of the ballad demanded a fixed length of line instead of the evidently freer chant of the epic. By the mid-16th century the double octosyllable had become established, though one still finds rare lines of 9, 7, and even 6 syllables. Whether we write our ballads down in long or short lines seems immaterial. The MSS from the earliest times (1421), and the 16th-century printers, use short lines, although long lines are used by Nebrija (1492) and by Salinas in his music-book (1577). Most modern editors use the short line (Menéndez y Pelayo in Spain and Le Strange in Britain are exceptions). Space-saving may sometimes be a consideration. Short lines are used here because they are more pleasing to the reader's eye, but more than that, because they seem better to express the rapidity and intense emotion of the texts.

It might be thought that the nature of the ballad tune would serve to resolve the doubt. Menéndez Pidal affirms that in the modern tradition the tune has a musical phrase of 16 (occasionally 32) notes, and it is said that British ballad tunes similarly have a long phrase. However, it seems that in the late 15th and 16th centuries in courtly Spanish performance as evidenced in the MS *Cancionero musical de la Colombina* and in printed works, there is a remarkable constancy of musical form. The settings are for a solo voice, or in some cases for three or four different voices (soprano, tenor, etc.). The pace was slow, there was a pause at the end of each octo- syllabic musical phrase, and everything points to the poems being considered as structured in short lines. There seems to have been no repetition and little adornment, though some was introduced by the *vihuelistas* of the mid-16th century in printed books.

Although the octosyllable has dominated for so long, it was not always so exclusive. There is plenty of evidence that in the 15th century a variety of strophic forms could be used for ballads and ballad-like poems, including octosyllables with full rhyme, couplets, ballads with refrains, etc. At the height of its popularity in the 16th century, however, when the power and coherence of the *Romancero* began to be perceived, collectors and editors and musicians came to feel that all true ballads should be in octosyllables, and most of the metrically variant forms were assimilated to this single pattern. Learned poets of the Golden Age occasionally experimented with ballads in diverse forms, and the six-syllable *romancillo* enjoyed a vogue (Góngora's examples are particularly charming), but these belong to the class of *romances artificiosos*. The *romancillo* had had a modest existence in popular tradition, the ballad of *Don Bueso* in this form being widespread (and still alive in Asturias, Morocco, and eastern Sephardic areas). Division into quatrains and the use of refrains seem unhappy variants in a genre whose special merit is freedom in extent and the power to flow on. (The division into paragraphs by sense, followed in this book, is arbitrary but reflects natural pauses.) The basic ballad form has never ceased to have an appeal for some of the greatest poets in the language despite so many other shifts of taste.[9]

(b) Structure and style

There is nothing primitive or uncouth about the structure and style of the ballads. Theirs is special art, evolved down the generations and found acceptable to the taste of many millions.

Most of the ballads are relatively short poems which deal with one scene, one episode, or one very closely linked series of events. In many cases nothing is said about the events which led up to the ballad-situation, even though this may result in some obscurity. Often too there is lacking that logical conclusion which modern readers might expect. This *fragmentismo* is a major feature of the Spanish ballads. As we have seen, some of the older ballads are reworked fragments of epics, or are in other ways related to an epic scene. These have in a way been removed from their contexts and have not been furnished with introductions and conclusions which might then seem necessary. Listeners and readers in the 16th century were still at least vaguely familiar with the surrounding contexts, and knew that in the ballad which starts

> 'Morir os queredes, padre,
> ¡San Miguel os haya el alma!' (No. 15)

the speaker is Princess Urraca and the father is King Ferdinand I. Moreover, this accident of *fragmentismo* was, by a collective stroke of genius, turned into a positive virtue when ballads of non-epic origin, such as No. 70, were treated, or perhaps originally composed, with the same criteria in view (see the Notes to No. 70). The modern reader need not feel unduly ignorant if notes are required to explain a ballad-situation. Towards the end of the 16th century one comes across versions which are much less abrupt, for to them introductory and explanatory matter has been added to aid the failing epic memories of listeners. The text quoted above is then made to start with the lines

> Por una sala adelante
> sañuda va doña Urraca;
> palabras iba diciendo
> que el corazón me quebranta:

which, though attractive in a way, greatly lessen the tension.

Stylistic consequences flow from this *fragmentismo*. The ballad is concise and compact, fast-moving, and not a word is wasted. The narration is simple and straightforward, in proper logical order, although it may take great leaps. The ballad states circumstances and facts, never motives, and it cannot pause to analyse the emotions of the participants. There is no room for the spaciousness and variety of incident of the epic. Static descriptions are kept to a minimum (but see below), and everything is

Introduction

concentrated upon the action and the words spoken, as the instinct of successive singers gets to work with what Menéndez Pidal calls its *enérgico esfuerzo depurador*. Adjectives are few, rarely of the kind called 'idle' (e.g. *green* grass). If there is a need for static description, a few features are mentioned and must serve to conjure up the rest in the imagination. So Diego Ordóñez goes out to his jousting

> de dobles piezas armado
> y en un caballo morcillo (No. 18)

The Carolingian and *fronterizo* ballads constitute important exceptions to this. Here the tone is more completely narrative, and there are quite full descriptions of places, dress, and movements, as the ballad seeks to impress the hearer with the exotic and the picturesque:

> Por esa puerta de Elvira
> sale muy gran cabalgada:
> ¡Cuánto del hidalgo moro!
> ¡Cuánta de la yegua baya!
> ¡Cuánta de la lanza en puño!
> ¡Cuánta de la adarga blanca! (No. 29)

At the opening of the ballad we are often taken up bodily and thrust into an action that is already well under way. A single line with a place-name may suffice to set the scene:

> En Burgos está el buen rey... (No. 25)
> Caballeros de Moclín... (No. 32)
> Por los caños de Carmona... (No. 45)

Or one of the protagonists may be abruptly named:

> Preso está Fernán González... (No. 77)
> Cabalga Diego Laínez... (No. 26)

Or more dramatically still, the protagonists may be directly addressed:

> 'Buen conde Fernán González...' (No. 9)
> 'Dadme nuevas, caballeros...' (No. 36)

But the most striking of ballad openings, and no doubt the most highly evolved, are those in which a speaker begins in direct speech, often a tirade, his or her name completely unannounced and perhaps not mentioned at all later in the text. Many of these are powerful exclamations, often reiterated:

> '¡Afuera, afuera, Rodrigo!...' (No. 16)
> '¡Oh Belerma, oh Belerma!...' (No. 53)

The ending of the ballad is of great importance too. A few have a somewhat weak and anticlimactic air (e.g. No. 20). Others have an extraordinary air of

xxxi

inevitability (e.g. Nos. 18, 34). In others the ending is plainly a temporary one, meant to lead thoughts on to a consequence or even to a ballad sequel, the next in the cycle (e.g. Nos. 10, 12, 15, 17). In many instances the endings show a fine instinct for understatement, for knowing when not to explain or insist, for *saber callar a tiempo* in Menéndez Pidal's phrase. The brevity and economy of narration might be not merely a poetic device but the reflection of an outlook on life, that of an austere people with a taste for the dramatic.

As noted earlier, most ballads have an impersonal viewpoint. In a few the *yo* intrudes, with a variety of possible effects. In some cases the protagonist himself is the narrator, so that the *yo* has a natural place (Nos. 59, 60, 69). In another the effect is to put a useful notion of distance between the observer and the scene described, giving an extra dimension:

> Por aquel postigo viejo
> que nunca fuera cerrado,
> *vi* venir pendón bermejo (No. 19)

Rather similar in intention is the apostrophe to the town, from an observer stationed outside and above it:

> Álora, la bien cercada,
> tú que estás en par del río (No. 34)

Such worthwhile effects might have been more widely adopted, but there were rather few precedents in the epic tradition for the direct intervention of the narrator.

If the narrator infrequently presents himself, the protagonists often express themselves in direct speech whose vigour can rarely be paralleled in other genres. It was natural that the ballads should inherit from (or share with) the epics the capacity for dramatisation in direct speech, for many of the best passages of the epics which were detached or adapted as ballads were of precisely this kind, and in essence the epic was as much drama as narrative. The direct speech is usually a dialogue, often a spirited dispute, sometimes a series of question-and-answer passages developed in parallel structures and involving antithesis, for which the ballad line seems to be specially effective (e.g. Nos. 8, 20, 64). There is a fine vigour about the way in which Moorish rulers issue instructions (Nos. 28, 29), lyricism in the occasional soliloquy (Nos. 3, 12, 69), and pathos in Doña Alda's account of her dream (No. 44). Sometimes the ballad consists entirely of direct speech (Nos. 16, 46, 69), and the ballad which is wholly narrative is rare (Nos. 4, 56). The balance between narrative and direct speech elements, the economy of the former and the power of the latter, the invariably neat way in which speakers are introduced and removed – these constitute one of the best achievements of the ballad genre.

Another notable feature of ballad-language is repetition, particularly in first lines. These can have an intensely dramatic effect. Some are exclamatory and imitate the repetitions of everyday speech at emotional moments:

> '¡Afuera, afuera, Rodrigo!...' (No. 16)
> '¡Abenámar, Abenámar!...'(No. 33)

Sometimes there is a note of quiet desperation:

> 'Que por mayo era, por mayo...' (No. 69)

and at others a solemn note of doom:

> '¡Rey don Sancho, rey don Sancho!...' (No. 17)

Narrative lines frequently use repetition too, as a means of underlining a significant point:

> Doliente estaba, doliente... (No. 14)

But it seems that very often the opening repetition is intended simply to have an incantatory effect, lifting our minds from everyday reality into a world of make-believe. Here the words have an insistent jingle in no way different from that of the nursery-rhymes which charmed us as children:

> Fontefrida, Fontefrida... (No. 61)
> 'Rosa fresca, Rosa fresca...' (No. 62)

Alliteration is frequently a part of this jingle, the sounds *m* and *c* (*k*) being the most favoured:

> Yo me era mora Moraima,
> morilla de un bel catar... (No. 59)
> Yo me adamé una amiga... (No. 60)
> La bella malmaridada... (No. 65)
> Por los caños de Carmona... (No. 45)
> En Castilla está un castillo ... (No. 48)

As the ballad develops there may be further repetitions, sometimes for necessary emphasis, but also because of the sheer musical appeal of a word or a line. There is poetry too in the very names of persons and places, those of the Carolingian ballads in particular having an exotic and possibly even erotic euphony (*Melisenda, Belerma*).

The language of the ballads is, in one way, of an extreme plainness, and helps to make them admirable texts for beginners in the language. A poem which is to be recited or sung must communicate its sense immediately, since there can be no pause for thought and no turning back the page. But there is more than this utilitarian reason for the ballad's simplicity: a desire to fix attention on the scene and its attendant emotions, not on any special beauties of language. Even so, the ballads are full of exquisite, pithy, or forceful lines which, aided by their music, stay in one's mind as permanent possessions. Brevity and neatness are constantly sought, and it is not surprising that a number of lines are listed as proverbs by Golden Age authorities such as Covarrubias (1611) and Correas (about 1630), while others were quoted in real life and in the drama because they summed up a situation and were known to all. Of the poetic figures commonly used in more sophisticated verse we find only simile in the ballads, and this is rare and, when used, simple in character.

In another sense the language of the ballads has its curiosities and complexities. Two factors must be borne in mind. One is that the ballad manner partook of much of the epic manner, and both genres were meant to be delivered orally by a performer to an audience. One finds in consequence a number of formulae dear to the hearts of the performers, the *juglares*. They are not mere fossils, because each serves a definable purpose, but it is plain that on occasion they are useful as line-fillers before the narrative takes its next step, and they also doubtless aided improvisation if memory failed or if a variant was being tried out. Such are

bien oiréis lo que dirá

which can be varied to fit assonances other than -á. This announces the start of a speech or a change of speaker, as it does in the *Poema de mio Cid* (e.g. line 70). A narrative formula for 'meanwhile' is

ellos en aquesto estando

which corresponds to line 2311 of the *Poema*. Both these involve a perhaps necessary slackening of the tension of the ballad. A formula intended to increase the tension is the apparently tautological but very vivid

llorando de los sus ojos

which is found on numerous occasions in the *Poema* (e.g. 1, 277), and in many other medieval texts. Other narrative devices taken over from or shared with epic enable the performer to bring a scene to life as though it were happening before the eyes of the audience. The lively opening to ballad No. 21, *Hélo, hélo, por do viene*, corresponds to the minstrel's *Afévos...* in the *Poema* (e.g. 152). The use of the 2nd plural *viérades* in No. 34 echoes the minstrel's address to his public (e.g. *Poema* 170), and what Menéndez Pidal calls the '*ya*' *actualizante* (e.g. No. 18) is similarly an aid to vivid narration (compare *Poema* 1448). Rather different is the device adopted in certain *fronterizo* ballads (e.g. No. 29) in which rapid phrases each starting with the exclamatory *¡Cuánto...!* try to impress a colourful and varied scene upon the listener's mind, in a way already known to the epic *juglares* (compare *Poema* 726-30). Readers acquainted with the epic texts will note in the ballads other features which show a community of tradition and outlook between the two.

Introduction

The apparent anarchy of the verb-tenses used in the ballads may alarm those brought up to a strict view of the matter. Historical presents, intended to make the action live again in the imagination, are common. For the rest, it is possible in some instances to agree with Menéndez Pidal, following Spitzer, that the deliberately vague time-sense of the ballads accords well with their geographical and historical vagueness. In many other cases liberties are taken with the logic of tenses because, as in the epic, freedom was necessary to secure a rhythm or an assonance, while in oral delivery such potential variability was helpful in improvisation. There is a full analysis by Szertiks (1967).

There is, finally, a strongly archaic flavour about much of ballad language. In part this is because Old Spanish elements were still living during the great vogue for ballads at the end of the 15th century and these were not too impossibly archaic when the texts were printed in the 16th. But in part too the archaisms were and are retained for entirely positive reasons, because of the great affection felt for them in so traditional a genre whose subject-matter may go back many centuries. Counts, princesses, Moorish rulers, and talking nightingales impose a certain dignity and non-ordinariness of language. The archaism can be spoken and sung no more self-consciously than it is, for example, in the English nursery-rhyme (*Whither shall I wander?*). In the verb-system one notices such Old Spanish features as *haber* meaning 'to possess', *ser* and *estar* not so clearly differentiated as in modern usage (with *estar* providing a necessary extra syllable at times), and the habit of forming the compound tenses of some verbs with *ser*. Commonly the *-ara* form of the verb, now a subjunctive, appears still in its Latin past-indicative sense (Latin pluperfect *amaveram*, *amaram: amara*), still common today as a survival or revival in subordinate clauses in literary and journalistic usage. Occasionally, as in the epic, the present subjunctive (e.g. *dígasme ora ese cantar*) or imperfect subjunctive (e.g. *prestásesme tu puñal*) are used as imperatives. Other archaic features are the use of the split future (e.g. *Dároslo he yo, mi señora*), the survival of the article beside the possessive (e.g. *los mis moricos, un vuestro servidor*), and the appearance of *ese* and other demonstratives in their very ancient function of definite articles (*e.g. ese buen rey don Fernando*). Archaic lexical items and forms are listed in the glossary.

The principle followed in printing the texts has been to modernise the spelling in every case where this could be done, since there seemed to be no point in maintaining the spelling *Ceupta*, for example (No. 1), as other modern editors often do. However, some archaic spellings must be retained for metrical reasons; thus, in the line:

Non era nada, mi fijo (No. 25)

non and *fijo* are so spelled for the correct syllable-count.

(c) Themes and sentiments

The ballads have a wide range of subjects. Given the relationship of many to the military feudal epic, one might expect a large number to deal with war, but outside the *fronterizo* group few actually describe battles (No. 41 is one). The Zamora ballads (Nos. 14-20) are not concerned with the siege as such, and the main point of *Las huestes de don Rodrigo* (No. 3) is not the fighting but the king's lament. It has been said that the masculine world and bloodthirstiness of the epic correspond to the rough solidity of Norman or Romanic architecture, whereas in the ballads we move into the gentler, more feminine and more delicate atmosphere of 15th-century Gothic.

In the older Castilian 'historical' ballads the themes are still feuds between noble families and disputes between king and vassal, but in the Carolingian and novelesque poems the favourite subjects are tense situations between lovers or between husband and wife. However, any theme having inherent dramatic qualities and allowing the development of vigorous question-and-answer can be used. The distinction between historical and novelesque ballads is a useful one here. In the historical, the small drama is played out by two protagonists against a background of larger events. Although they are not mentioned specifically, we are aware that in the wider area just outside our view courtiers and retainers are present, armies are deployed, siege-towers rise, and the fate of cities and kingdoms is being decided. Nationally-known places and persons are mentioned, giving an air of historical reality, even though there is no insistence upon these facts (and any 'facts' may be no more than pseudo-history or legend anyway). Even so, the broad sweep of the epic is forgotten and its grandeur is diminished. We are no longer interested in the Cid's total achievement, but in a series of picturesque personal incidents. Although the Franks still fight for Christian Europe and Roland still embodies the feudal virtues in *Ya comienzan los franceses* (No. 41), we are more likely to remember Doña Alda alone with her terrifying dream (No. 44).

Sentimental incidents are developed out of the military action of the parent epic. The ballad *¡Afuera, afuera, Rodrigo!* (No. 16) is an altogether fictitious development, based on the fact that in the epic of Zamora it was briefly said that Urraca and the Cid had known each other as children. Jimena has a whole new cycle of ballads about equally fictitious aspects of her affair with the Cid. But even here we are still aware of the broad backcloth, of the far-reaching consequences of the small scene before our eyes. In the novelesque ballads, on the other hand, there is none of this: only the protagonists are and will be concerned. Place-names are rarely mentioned and are quite superfluous. Protagonists have melodious but unlikely names: *Melisenda, Rosa fresca* (but there was a famous Mélisende, Queen of Jerusalem 1131-61). We cannot think of an historical time and setting even if we try.

A further important division in the themes follows from this. Most of the Castilian ballads, despite their vagueness (in comparison with the epic) and their tendency towards sentimentality, preserve a sober down-to-earth attitude. It is pointless to talk of 'realism'; but the people are credible and the things that happen to them are feasible. Even the bloody tale of the Infantes de Lara is perfectly credible, given the fierce habits of early medieval clans when dealing with offences against honour. In the Carolingian ballads, however, we move into a different world. Here are magic and mystery, significant numbers, sexual symbols, dreams, fairy castles, in short, something more akin to that fantastic image which the Middle Ages easily implant in modern minds.[10] The novelesque ballads partake of both tendencies, depending on their origins: Moraima (No. 59) lives in a very real southern Spanish street, and the Prisoner (No. 69) in any real prison; but Conde Arnaldos (No. 70) comes from remote, romantic France, and has possibly had a sojourn in fairyland.

While most ballads are concerned with scenes and people for their own poetic sake, two more general themes do emerge. One is justice, a proper retribution for wrongs committed. In the tale of the Infantes de Lara justice is exacted privately and bloodily. If the matter is put to the king, in a king-and-vassal situation so typical of epic and ballad, the ballad usually takes the side of the vassal, the king being shown as either unjust (to Bernardo del Carpio and Fernán González) or ineffective (the Cid and Jimena).

The second general theme is simply that life is tragic. In the poems about King Roderick and in the Zamora group, we have the makings of great tragedies: human failings have the direst consequences, and events follow each other with a dour inevitability. People are painted in their true undistinguished grey, rather than in villainous black and saintly white, and there are no heroes. This tragic sense is strongly present too in the *fronterizo* ballads, and is enhanced by the refusal to indulge in moralising sentiments or to add 'they lived happily ever after' endings.

The ballads have their own simple morality in sexual matters. Their attitude to crimes of lust ('crime' seems a better word than 'sin', because the ballads are wholly unecclesiastical in tone and rarely use the word *pecado*) is interesting and varied. The Castilian ballads are somewhat puritanical and do not deal with situations of this kind for the most part, and this itself is significant. But there are exceptions: King Roderick seduces La Cava and loses his realm and his life in consequence (and in other poems survives to do a particularly horrifying penance); No. 7, in which a lustful archpriest is punished. In No. 16, a very shifty Cid mentions the possibility of divorcing Jimena if Princess Urraca still wishes to marry him, as she has brazenly implied. Some of the Carolingian and Breton ballads, in contrast to the Castilian, deal with sexual matters as favourite themes, and in a surprisingly amoral way. The women personages advertise their charms and seem to be without scruple. Illicit love goes unpunished in many cases and even uncriticised. Some of these ballads were provided with suitably moral endings in the prudish days of the later 16th century: Gerineldos marries the princess, and a bishop is called in to marry Melisenda and Ayuelos, but they are not taxed with any crime or sin. The two ballads about the unhappily married girl (Nos. 64 and 65) have, in our versions, highly moral endings, but the notes to No. 64 draw attention to the disparity of treatments of this theme in different cultures. A variety of attitudes to sexual licence is displayed in the ballad of Conde Claros, No. 54, the archbishop and the nuns being among those who beg the king to pardon the less-than-errant Count. The ballads, in short, owe surprisingly little to church teaching, and flourished in song and in print in a long period (the 16th and 17th centuries) when the Inquisition and an at least outward puritanism were so powerful in Spain. The ballads are far too from the artificial and brutal standards of the Golden Age *drama de honor*. No Calderonian father, discovering a page-boy in bed with his daughter, would have been content merely to lay a sword between them, and in silence too (No. 55). The Spanish collectivity seems to have had plenty of common sense and human sympathy and gave voice to these in its ballads.[11]

Themes and sentiments are naturally those selected by the original poet, modified or exaggerated or even wholly reinterpreted by the *autor-legión*. It is assumed that the original poets and early performers were, like the 16th-century printers and the composers of *romances artificiosos*, men. However, the modern oral tradition in all societies seems to belong – as memory and in performance – largely, though far from exclusively (Michael, 1996) has some statistics), to women and to the tradition of women's lore in the family and the social group. Themes and sentiments in the living *romancero* of recent times must therefore respond in some measure to women's concerns and feelings. This has hardly been discussed as yet, but an admirable start is made in the 1990 paper by Teresa Catarella.

5. THE SPANISH BALLADS IN BRITAIN AND THE UNITED STATES

British and American scholars and poet-translators have, beside the Germans mentioned earlier (3b above) an honourable place in the history of the Spanish ballads. It is likely that the ballads first attracted attention because they figure so largely in *Don Quixote*, a favourite book with 18th-century readers in England. In the notes to his translation of *Don Quixote* (1781) the Rev. John Bowle shows a direct acquaintance with a

number of Spanish ballad anthologies, and in 1812 Thomas Rodd publish-
ed texts and translations of 22 ballads mentioned in Cervantes' book. There
is evidence that readers in Britain were drawn to the romanticism of the
Moorish poems even earlier, however. They knew these through Pérez de
Hita's *Guerras civiles de Granada* (1595), which seems to have been
widely known in the original or in French versions during the 18th century.
The Moorish ballads were mentioned as true examples of popular poetry
by Thomas Blackwell in a contribution to the Homer debate (1735).
Thomas Percy translated two of Pérez de Hita's ballads in his *Reliques of
Ancient English Poetry* (1765) and began to work on others from the same
source in his *Ancient Songs chiefly on Moorish Subjects translated from
the Spanish* (1775, but not printed till 1932). Thomas Rodd published
translations of ballads in the Pérez de Hita book in 1801, and in 1803
translated the whole novel.

Of much greater importance was the interest taken in the *romancero* as
a whole by some of the leading writers of the Romantic movement in
Britain, for whom, as for the French and German Romantics, the spirit,
colourfulness, and exotic notes of the ballads had great appeal. At first
matters were not helped by the opinion of Robert Southey (1808), a fine
Hispanist, who translated the *Chronicle of the Cid* and some *fronterizo*
poems, that the ballads did not deserve their high reputation and were much
inferior to their Scottish counterparts. This view did not long prevail. There
were versions of a few ballads by Byron, Scott, and Lord Holland, but the
real fame of the Spanish ballads in Britain began when John Gibson
Lockhart (1794-1854) published his translations in parts in *Blackwood's
Magazine* in 1822 and issued them in book form as *Ancient Spanish
Ballads, Historical and Romantic* in 1823. Lockhart was a considerable
literary figure as editor, reviewer, novelist, and poet. He was married to
Scott's daughter Sophia and wrote a famous *Life* of the great novelist, and
he edited the *Quarterly Review* from 1825 to 1853. His collection of ballad
translations was enthusiastically received by *Blackwood's Magazine* and
the *Edinburgh Review* in long review-articles which praised Lockhart's
versions and expressed admiration for the originals. The latter were
esteemed for their simplicity, freedom from excessive adornment, and (in
comparison with the Scottish ballads) refinement of tone. They were
admired too – often mistakenly, as we now know – for their archaic and
genuinely popular quality. Lockhart's collection, with an interesting intro-
duction and scholarly notes, included some 50 poems drawn from all
groups and arranged in chronological order of the events they describe, as
in Depping's edition of 1817. His choice is sometimes faulty, however: he
has good *morisco* and *fronterizo* texts, but his Cid ballads are poor ones
and he has none about Zamora. Although Macaulay declared Lockhart's
translations superior to their originals, it is now plain that his knowledge

of Spanish was far from perfect, and some of his mistranslations have aroused the ire of Spaniards. He took unjustified liberties with his texts, embroidering the plain originals with bright threads of rhetoric and archaism which are to be regretted. This is how he starts his version of *Que por mayo era, por mayo* (No. 69):

'Tis now, they say, the month of May, 'tis now the moons
are bright;
'Tis now the maids, 'mong greenwood shades, sit with
their loves by night

But he could do better, as in his translation of *En París está doña Alda* (No. 44):

In Paris sits the lady that shall be Sir Roland's bride,
Three hundred damsels with her, her bidding to abide

All this was much to the taste of contemporaries. Lockhart's ballads, sometimes in beautiful editions with romantic engravings, were very widely read, and went into nine editions by 1890. They were so well known they were thought worth parodying: 'Bon Gaultier' (Martin & Aytoun) composed three pseudo-Lockhart poems, *The Broken Pitcher* (mock-Moorish), *Don Fernando Gomersalez*, and *The Courtship of our Cid*, which occupy the first places in the collected *Bon Gaultier Ballads* (1845, and in its 17th edition by 1904). Martin declared that 'Lockhart's *Spanish Ballads* were as familiar in the drawing-room as in the study', and they seem as much a part of the Victorian scene as purple velvet and *The Monarch of the Glen*.

Another collection of some forty ballad translations by Sir John Bowring, *Ancient Poetry and Romances of Spain* (1824) seems to have received less wide approval, despite the interest of Bowring's effort to render the texts into a sort of English assonance. Finally one notes the much more faithful but less spirited renderings by the Rev. J.Y. Gibson in *The Cid Ballads, and other Poems and Translations from Spanish and German* (1887, 2nd ed. 1898).

It will be noted that while the ballads were, thanks largely to Lockhart, probably more widely known in Britain than in Germany, British scholars contributed nothing much to the study of the ballads which was being so brilliantly begun in Germany and other countries. Even Lockhart's introductory essay has nothing to say on the matter of ballad origins, and is very inexact on the subject of metrics. Lockhart did however recognise that the ballads 'form by far the oldest, as well as the largest, collection of popular poetry, properly so called, that is to be found in the literature of any European nation whatever'. He noted that neoclassical taste persisted in the Spain of his day, and urged the Spaniards to pay due attention to their heritage: 'While hundreds of volumes have been written about authors who were, at the best, ingenious imitators of classical or Italian models, not one, of the least critical merit, has been bestowed upon these older and simpler poets who were contented with the native inspirations of Castilian pride.'

Independent criticism of the ballads in the United States began with Longfellow's essay 'Ancient Spanish Ballads' in his book *Outre-Mer* of 1833, but this is a brief general appreciation rather than a scholarly investigation. Longfellow included three spirited translations in the essay, and quoted others by Lockhart and Byron; the American's are far superior, and lead one to regret that he did not carry this work further. The poem which was inspired by *¡Quién hubiese tal ventura!* – one cannot call it a translation – will be mentioned in its place (No. 70). Other translations, of an explanatory rather than a literary kind, are given by G. Ticknor in his great *History of Spanish Literature* (1849), which contains a study of the ballads better than anything published up to that time.

In our century the attempts to translate the ballads into English have not had the impact of Lockhart's. It may in any case be assumed that a knowledge of Spanish is now more widespread in English-speaking countries. Also the difficulty of doing justice to such deceptively plain originals has perhaps been recognised and has deterred translators. However, Samuel Armistead in his helpful review of the first edition of this book rightly commented that a statement about this was too negative, and it is proper to recall *Some Spanish Ballads* by the American W.S. Merwin (1961) and in Britain the well-known anthology by J.M. Cohen, *The Penguin Book of Spanish Verse* (1956 and later editions), which includes more than 30 pages of ballads.[12] Roger Wright's lively versions (1987) are probably unique in that they are not merely intended for public performance but have been sung by their author to his own guitar accompaniment.

The scholars who carried on the study of the British ballads so admirably – Child, Kittredge, Gummere, Gerould, and others – seem on the whole to have been unaware of how much the Spanish tradition had to offer them. It was left to W.J. Entwistle of Oxford, a Hispanist chiefly, but an expert in several fields, to take the necessary broad view in his *European Balladry* (1939). He also wrote many specialised studies of the Spanish epic and ballad. Work by more recent American and British Hispanists is mentioned in the Classified Booklist and in the notes to the texts.

6. THE PRESENT EDITION

No claim can be made for the originality of the selection of these 70 ballads. Most are taken from the *Primavera y flor de romances* published by Wolf and Hofmann in 1856, in its second edition by Menéndez y Pelayo in 1899, and a few – Nos. 27, 40, 41, 45, 55, 68 – are taken from the

Appendices in which Menéndez y Pelayo added texts to the original *Primavera*. To take the ballads from this single source, as others have done, was obviously convenient. But there is more justification than that: the *Primavera*, based in the main on the *cancioneros de romances* of the mid-16th century, contains the best of the traditional *Romancero* set down at the height of its popularity (as gauged by the sales anticipated by printers) at the moment when, by common consent, it had reached perfection. It has thus been possible to take this collection as a representative corpus and study it in a variety of ways. But as noted earlier, it is far from correct to regard this mid-16th corpus as 'the' *Romancero* in any exclusive way. For one thing, enormous quantities of materials have been added to it since then from authors popular and learned, and for another, recorders and scholars of the modern oral tradition in several Hispanic languages and many countries have used their materials to illustrate the workings of a traditional and orally-transmitted genre, their principles and findings often being applicable to the conjectured evolution of the ballads before the 16th century. It is certain that due account of modern orality is not taken in this book, which has a quite different purpose, but by way of modest adjustment a section about it has been added to the Booklist.

In selecting 70 texts from the 198 of the *Primavera* and others added by Menéndez y Pelayo, two criteria were applied: that there should be representatives of most groups of the *romances viejos* and a few of the *juglarescos*, and that their poetic quality should be high. Most of the texts are in consequence similar to those published in other small anthologies, but this is not a disadvantage, since the reader will be assimilating an important part of that poetic culture which is (through such editions in our century) common to Spanish speakers in many countries.

The spelling of the texts has been modernised in all cases, except (as explained in 4b above) where archaic forms must be retained for metrical reasons. Accents have been supplied, and some liberty has been taken with punctuation. Quotation marks replace the dash used by Spanish printers. Some division into 'paragraphs' has been attempted in keeping with the sense.

Any titles that could be assigned to the ballads would be purely arbitrary; the best way of referring to them is by their first lines, and they are indexed in this way.

NOTES TO THE INTRODUCTION

1. Sir Walter Scott, who printed most of the known Scottish ballads in his collection *Minstrelsy of the Scottish Border* (1802-3), was told by Mrs Hogg: 'There war never ane o' my sangs prentit till ye prentit them yoursel', an' ye hae spoilt them awthegither. They were made for singing an' no for reading; but ye hae broken the charm now, an' they'll never be sung mair' (quoted by W. Beattie, *Border Ballads* (Harmondsworth: Penguin, 1952), p. 16).

2. The English *ballad* derives from the Old French *balade* and Occitan *balada* 'dancing-song', from late Latin *ballare* 'to dance'; but there seems to be no connection between the known British ballads and dancing. The word appears in English from the late 15th century (*OED*). In modern Spanish *balada* appears as a loanword from the mid-19th century with reference to ballads outside Spain. One modern French word for a popular ballad or lovesong is *romance* (fem.), borrowed from Spanish, and modern French collections of ballads have been entitled *Romancéro*. From the Spanish there also derives the Italian *romanza*, which as a musical term has passed back into Spanish. Our English word *romance* in its variety of senses derives via Norman French from the same Latin root *romanice*.

3. See P. Bénichou, 'Romancero español y romanticismo francés', in *Hispanic Studies in Honor of Joseph H. Silverman* (Newark, Delaware: Juan de la Cuesta, 1988), 77-106.

4. R. Wright, 'How Old is the Ballad Genre?', *La Corónica* 14 (1985-6) 251-7, and 'Several Ballads, One Epic and Two Chronicles (1100-1250)', *La Corónica* 18 (1989-90) 21-38. The articles are reproduced, with brief postscripts, in Wright's book *Early Ibero-Romance* (Newark, Delaware: Juan de la Cuesta, 1994), 289-98 and 299-318. The other references are to C. Smith, 'The Variant Version of the Start of the *Poema de mio Cid*', *La Corónica* 20 (1991-2) 32-41, and S.G. Armistead, '*Encore les cantilènes!* Prof. Roger Wright's *Proto-Romances*', *La Corónica* 15 (1986-7) 52-66.

5. As in E.M. Wilson's expert definition, in his review in *Bulletin of Hispanic Studies* 42 (1965) 186.

6. Sancho implies that 'las trovas de los romances antiguos no mienten' when he tells an unlikely tale of King Roderick, and is supported in this by Doña Rodríguez; but the Duchess laughs and has her doubts (II, 33).

7. In his *Avertissement*, written to justify his construction of the play and his handling of 'history', Corneille quotes the historian Mariana on the Cid's marriage and then two ballads, whose authority he tries to

establish by saying that 'ces sortes de petits poèmes sont comme des originaux décousus de leurs anciennes histoires'. Both ballads are, however, not *viejos*, still less epic fragments, but of late 16th-century date.

8. See their notice of the first edition of this book in *Hispanic Review* 37 (1969) 407-12 (408).

9. Lope de Vega, one of the finest composers of *romances artificiosos*, was not ashamed to include a couple of them among his more erudite verse in Italianate metres when he published a collection of his *Rimas* in 1604. His preface contains this justification: 'Romances no me puedo persuadir que desdigan de la autoridad de las *Rimas*, aunque se atreve a su facilidad la gente ignorante porque no se obligan a la corresponsión de las cadencias. Algunos quieren que sean la cartilla de los poetas [i.e., poets' primers or elementary schoolbooks]; yo no lo siento así, antes bien los hallo capaces, no sólo de exprimir y declarar cualquier concepto con fácil dulzura, pero de proseguir toda grave acción de numeroso poema. Y soy tan de veras español que, por ser en nuestro idioma natural este género, no me puedo persuadir que no sea digno de toda estimación' (quoted by Menéndez Pidal, *Rom. hisp.* II, 159-60).

10. This feeling for the supernatural is strongly present in many of the Scottish ballads. In them, however, it pervades the whole poem, whereas in the Carolingian ballads of Spain the supernatural is mostly present as an incidental only.

11. For more detailed discussion, see Smith (1972).

12. The Armistead-Silverman review mentioned in Note 8 adds further details of English translations, and studies of these. See also Bryant (1973).

CLASSIFIED BOOKLIST

Sections 2 to 5 correspond to sections in the Introduction. Chapters in general histories of literature are not listed, but it is proper to make an exception for the section 'El romancero' in Alan Deyermond's volume *Edad Media*, the first in the series *Historia y crítica de la literatura española* directed by Francisco Rico (Barcelona: Crítica, 1979), 255-64. Deyermond published a *Primer suplemento* to this volume in 1991, the section on ballads occupying pp. 209-34. In each case there is an expert survey of recent research, extensive bibliography, and reprints of notable essays by others.

Readers will find below a selection of major works, each in most cases providing a substantial list of specialist studies. In the introduction to each section of ballad texts other such indications will be found, and in the note of 'References' after each ballad one indication or more of the same kind. Roger Wright's *Critical Guide* has many too.

1. Texts

Early printings: Nucio's *Cancionero de romances* of Antwerp, often called the '*sin año*' (about 1548) was reproduced by R. Menéndez Pidal (Madrid: Junta para Ampliación de Estudios, 1914; second ed., Madrid: CSIC, 1945). Nucio's second edition, 1550, is reproduced with a study by A. Rodríguez-Moñino (Madrid: Castalia, 1967). The *Romancero general*, first published in parts in 1600, 1604, and 1605, was edited by A. González Palencia in two vols (Madrid: CSIC, 1947), and its sources and originals (facsimiles of the most important *romanceros* published from 1589 to 1597) were traced by A. Rodríguez-Moñino in *Las fuentes del Romancero general* (Madrid: Real Academia Española, 1957-71, 12 vols). On the *pliegos sueltos*, the best source is A. Rodríguez-Moñino, *Diccionario de pliegos sueltos poéticos (siglo XVI)* (Madrid: Castalia, 1970).

A collection much used in the 19th century was that of A. Durán, *Romancero general, o colección de romances castellanos anteriores al siglo XVIII*, vols X (1849) and XVI (1851) of the *Biblioteca de Autores Españoles* published by Rivadeneyra. The *Primavera y flor de romances* edited by F.J. Wolf and C. Hofmann (Berlin: Asher, 1856) became well known in Spain when it was reissued, with additions, by M. Menéndez y Pelayo as vols VIII and IX of his *Antología de poetas líricos castellanos* (Madrid: Biblioteca Clásica, 1899), these being reproduced as vols XXIV and XXV of the *Edición nacional de las obras completas de...* (Santander: CSIC, 1945). The most-used small collection of recent times has been that of R. Menéndez Pidal, *Flor nueva de romances viejos* (Madrid: La Lectura,

1928), especially since 1938 in the Colección Austral (No. 100). A larger anthology is that of L. Santullano (Madrid: Aguilar, 1935, and later eds). Other collections are those of J. Alcina Franch, *Romancero antiguo* (Barcelona: Juventud, 2 vols, 1961-71). Among several anthologies of recent decades that of G. Di Stefano, *Romancero* (Madrid: Taurus, 1993) is outstanding, with 161 texts reproduced in strict accordance with original sources, expert commentary and good bibliography. The major modern source for texts and detailed studies is the *Romancero tradicional de las lenguas hispánicas (español-portugués-catalán-safardí)* begun in 1957 by Menéndez Pidal and continued by others, published in Madrid by the Seminario Menéndez Pidal and Gredos, 12 vols to 1985; individual volumes are referred to in the notes to groups of ballads below.

2. European Balladry and the Spanish *Romancero*

Bold, A., *The Ballad*, The Critical Idiom, 41 (London: Methuen, 1979)
Child, F.J., *The English and Scottish Popular Ballads*, 5 vols (1857-9; repr. New York: Folklore Press and Pageant Book Company, 1957)
Entwistle, W.J., *European Balladry*, 2nd ed. (Oxford: Clarendon, 1951)
Fowler, D.C., *A Literary History of the Popular Ballad* (Durham: North Carolina: Duke University Press, 1968)
Gerould, G.H., *The Ballad of Tradition* (Oxford, 1932; repr. New York: Dover Books, 1957)
Menéndez y Pelayo, M., *Tratado de los romances viejos*, in *Antología de poetas líricos castellanos* (Madrid: Biblioteca Clásica), vols XI (1903) and XII (1906); reprinted as vols XXII and XXIII of the *Edición nacional de las obras completas de* ... (Santander: CSIC, 1944)
Menéndez Pidal, R., *El romancero español* (New York: Hispanic Society, 1910; reprinted in *Estudios...*, 1973, 7-48)
Menéndez Pidal, R., *Romancero hispánico (hispano-portugués, americano y sefardí)*, 2 vols (Madrid: Espasa-Calpe, 1953)
Michaëlis de Vasconcellos, C., *Estudos sobre o romanceiro peninsular: Romances velhos em Portugal*, 2nd ed. (Coimbra, 1934; repr. Oporto: Lello & Irmao, 1980)
Rogers, E.R., *The Perilous Hunt: Symbols in Hispanic and European Balladry* (Lexington: University Press of Kentucky, 1980)

3. The History of the Spanish Ballads

(a) The name *romance*

Rom. hisp. I, 3-8
Garci-Gómez, M., '*Romance* según los textos españoles del medioevo y prerrenacimiento', *Journal of Medieval and Renaissance Studies* 4 (1974) 35-62

(b) Origins and development

Alvar, M., *El romancero: tradicionalidad y pervivencia*, 2nd ed. (Barcelona: Planeta, 1974)

Armistead, S.G., 'Neo-individualism and the *Romancero*', *Romance Philology* 33 (1979-80) 172-81

Atkinson, W.C., 'The Chronology of Spanish Ballad Origins', *Modern Language Review* 32 (1937) 44-61

Bénichou, P., *Creación poética en el romancero tradicional* (Madrid: Gredos, 1968)

Catalán, D., *Siete siglos de romancero* (Madrid: Gredos, 1969)

Di Stefano, G., *Sincronia e diacronia nel Romanzero* (Pisa: Università di Pisa, 1967)

Foster, D.W., *The Early Spanish Ballad*, Twayne's World Authors Series, 185 (New York: Twayne, 1971)

Menéndez Pidal, R., *Obras completas*, XI: *Estudios sobre el romancero* (Madrid: Espasa-Calpe, 1973). This contains many of his classic studies and much new work)

Michael, I., 'Factitious Flowers or Fictitious Fossils? The *romances viejos* Re-viewed', in B. Powell & G. West (eds), *'Al que en buen hora naçio' : Essays on the Spanish Epic and Ballad in Honour of Colin Smith* (Liverpool: Liverpool UP and MHRA, 1996) 91-105

(c) The ballads in the 15th century and the Golden Age

Rom. hisp. II, chs XI-XIV.

Aubrun, C.V., *Les vieux romances espagnols (1450-1550)* (Paris: Éditions Hispaniques, 1986)

Clarke, D.C., 'The Marqués de Santillana and the Spanish Ballad Problem', *Modern Philology* 59 (1961) 13-24, with full bibliography

Di Stefano, G., 'La difusión impresa del romancero antiguo en el siglo XVI', *Revista de Dialectología y Tradiciones Populares* 33 (1977) 373-411

Eisenberg, D., 'The *Romance* as seen by Cervantes', *El Crotalón* 1 (1984) 177-92; in Spanish in his book *Estudios cervantinos* (Barcelona: Sirmio, 1991), 57-82

Livermore, H.V., 'The 15th-century Evolution of the *Romance*', *Ibero-romania* 23 (1986) 20-39

Menéndez Pidal, R., & W. Starkie, *The Spaniards in their History* (London: Hollis & Carter, 1950) (ch. X, 'The Ballads and Don Quixote'; ch. XI, 'The Ballads and the Drama of the Golden Age')

Piacentini, G., *Ensayo de una bibliografía analítica del romancero antiguo: Los textos (siglos XV y XVI)*, 3 vols (Pisa: Giardini, 1981-93) (I, *Pliegos sueltos*; II, *Cancioneros y romanceros*; III, *Manuscritos*)

Tiemann, B., '*Aquellos siglos dorados*: Die Sammlungen der Cid-Romanzen: Ihre Herausbildung in Spanien und ihre Aufnahme im Ancien Régime Frankreichs', *Romanistisches Jahrbuch* 24 (1973) 241-93

(d) The ballads in modern times

In Spain: On the Civil War ballads, see S.M. Hart, 'Some Notes on the Conventions of Spanish Civil War Poetry: the *romance*', in M.A. Rees (ed.), *Leeds Papers on Lorca and on Civil War Verse* (Leeds: Trinity and All Saints' College, 1988), 109-28, with bibliography. Nobody has yet ventured a study of the sub-literary *romance* used in advertising jingles, local celebrations and festivities, scabrous ditties, political satire, and the like, but it would be well worth undertaking as a tribute to the persistent vigour of the genre. Examples of the now numerous collections from the regions of the Peninsula are: J.M. de Cossío & T. Maza Solano, *Romancero popular de la Montaña*, 2 vols (Santander: Sociedad de Menéndez y Pelayo, 1933-4); L. Díaz Viana & J. Díaz, *Romancero tradicional soriano*, 2 vols (Soria: Diputación Provincial, 1983); M.J. Ruiz Fernández, *El romancero tradicional de Jerez* (Jerez: Caja de Ahorros, 1991); Maximiano Trapero, *Romancero tradicional canario* (Las Palmas: Viceconsejería de Cultura y Deportes, 1989, with mention of earlier publications on ballads from various of the Canary Is., 1982-7).

In America: *Rom. hisp.* II, 341-56; R. Menéndez Pidal, *Los romances de América y otros estudios*, 4th ed. (Buenos Aires & Mexico: Espasa-Calpe Argentina, 1945). There are collections of texts from a number of regions and countries, for example A.M. Espinosa, *Romancero de Nuevo Méjico* (Madrid: CSIC, 1953); G. Beutler, *Estudios sobre el romancero español en Colombia* (Bogotá: Instituto Caro y Cuervo, 1977); M.S. de Cruz-Sáenz, *El romancero tradicional de Costa Rica* (Newark, Delaware: Juan de la Cuesta, 1986); M. Díaz Roig, *Romancero tradicional de América* (Mexico: El Colegio de México, 1990); see also M.E. Simmons, *A Bibliography of the 'Romance' and Related Forms in Spanish America* (Bloomington, 1963; repr. Westport, Conn.: Greenwood Press, 1972).

Sephardic tradition: *Rom. hisp.* II, 330-41; P. Bénichou, *Romances judeo-españoles de Marruecos*, 2nd edn, (Madrid: Castalia, 1968); S.G. Armistead & J.H. Silverman, *Tres calas en el romancero sefardí (Rodas, Jerusalén, Estados Unidos)* (Madrid: Castalia, 1979); and especially S.G. Armistead, *El romancero judeo-español en el Archivo Menéndez Pidal*, 3 vols (Madrid: Cátedra & Seminario Menéndez Pidal, 1978), being vols I-III in the series *Fuentes para el estudio del romancero: Serie sefardí*; earlier (1977), but numbered IV in the series, Armistead & Silverman edited *Romances judeo-españoles de Tánger recogidos por Zarita Nahón*; vol. V in the set is R. Benmayor (ed.), *Romances judeo-españoles de Oriente: nueva recolección* (1979).

On the modern oral tradition in general, in addition to the collections from the regions of the Peninsula, America, and the Sephardim mentioned above, a few outstanding titles must be selected from a huge range: *Rom. hisp.* II, chs XVIII-XXII; R. Menéndez Pidal, 'Sobre geografía folklórica: Ensayo de un método', *Revista de Filología Española* 7 (1920), 229-328, reprinted in *Estudios...* (1973), 217-323, and reworked by A. Galmés de Fuentes & D. Catalán as *Cómo vive un romance: Dos ensayos sobre tradicionalidad* (Madrid: CSIC, 1954); S.G. Armistead and others (eds), *El romancero hoy*, 3 vols (Madrid: Cátedra & Seminario Menéndez Pidal, 1979); D. Catalán and others, *El romancero pan-hispánico: Catálogo general descriptivo*, 3 vols (Gredos & Seminario Menéndez Pidal, 1982-4), which in vol. I (*Teoría general y metodología*) offers an indispensable general analysis of ballad structure and style, and in vols II & III the application of this to the 'Romances de contexto histórico nacional'; *Hispanic Balladry Today*, an issue of the journal *Oral Tradition* 2 (1987), revised and edited as a book by R.H. Webber (New York & London: Garland, 1989), with specially valuable contributions by S. Petersen ('In Defense of *Romancero* Geography', 74-115) and J. Seeger ('The Living Ballad in Brazil: Two Performances', 175-217); numerous papers gathered in *El romancero: Tradición y pervivencia a fines del siglo XX*, being *Actas del IV Coloquio Internacional del Romancero* [1987] (Cadiz: Fundación Machado & Universidad de Cádiz, 1991). There is a *Bibliografía del romancero oral*, I (Madrid: Cátedra & Seminario Menéndez Pidal, 1980).

4. The art of the Spanish ballads

(a) Form

Rom. hisp. I, ch. IV

Devoto, D., 'Sobre la métrica de los romances según el Romancero hispánico', *Cahiers de Linguistique Hispanique Médiévale* 4 (1979) 5-50

Gornall, J.F.G., 'Assonance in the Hispanic *Romance*: Precept and Practice', *Modern Language Review* 90 (1995) 363-9

(b) Structure and style

Rom. hisp. I, ch. III

Catalán, D., and others, *El romancero pan-hispánico: Catálogo general descriptivo*, I: *Teoría general y metodología* (Madrid: Gredos & Seminario Menéndez Pidal, 1984)
Chevalier, J.-C., 'Architecture temporelle du *Romancero tradicional*', *Bulletin Hispanique* 73 (1971) 50-103
Díaz Roig, M., *El romancero y la lírica popular moderna* (Mexico: Colegio de México, 1976)
Gilman, S., 'On *Romancero* as a Poetic Language', in *Crítica y poesía: Homenaje a Casalduero...* (Madrid: Gredos, 1972), 151-60
Lapesa, R., 'La lengua de la poesía épica en los cantares de gesta y en el romancero viejo', *Anuario de Letras* [Mexico] 4 (1964) 5-24, reprinted in his book *De la Edad Media a nuestros días: Estudios de historia literaria* (Madrid: Gredos, 1967), 9-28
Mirrer-Singer, L., 'The Characteristic Patterning of *Romancero* Language: Some Notes on Tense and Aspect in the *Romances viejos*', *Hispanic Review* 55 (1987) 441-61
Ochrymowycz, O.R., *Aspects of Oral Style in the 'Romances juglarescos' of the Carolingian Cycle* (Iowa City: University of Iowa, 1975)
Sandmann, M., 'La "mezcla de los tiempos narrativos" en el romancero viejo', *Romanistisches Jahrbuch* 25 (1974) 278-93
Szertics, J., *Tiempo y verbo en el romancero viejo* (Madrid: Gredos, 1967)
Webber, R.H., 'Formulistic Diction in the Spanish Ballad', *University of California Publications in Modern Philology* 34 (1951) 175-278

(c) Themes and sentiments

Catarella, T., 'Feminine Historicizing in the *romancero novelesco*', *Bulletin of Hispanic Studies* 67 (1990) 331-43
Devoto, D., 'Sobre el estudio folklórico del romancero español', *Bulletin Hispanique* 57 (1955) 233-91
Smith, C., 'On the Ethos of the *Romancero viejo*', in N.D. Shergold (ed.), *Studies of the Spanish and Portuguese Ballad* (London: Tamesis, 1972), 5-24
Smith, C., 'The Cid in Epic and Ballad', *European Writers. The Middle Ages and the Renaissance* (New York: Scribner, 1983), I, 113-36
Wilson, E.M., *Tragic Themes in Spanish Ballads* (London: Hispanic & Luso-Brazilian Councils, 1958); translated in his book *Entre las jarchas y Cernuda: Constantes y variables en la poesía española* (Barcelona: Ariel, 1977), 109-29

5. The Spanish Ballads in Britain and the United States

Bryant, S.M., *The Spanish Ballad in English* (Lexington: University Press of Kentucky, 1973)

6. Music

Martínez Torner, E., 'Indicaciones prácticas sobre la notación musical de los romances', *Revista de Filología Española* 10 (1923) 389-94

Martínez Torner, E., 'Ensayo de clasificación de las melodías de romance', *Homenaje a Menéndez Pidal* (Madrid: Hernando, 1925), II, 391-402

Sage, J., 'Early Spanish Ballad Music: Tradition or Metamorphosis?', in *Medieval Hispanic Studies presented to Rita Hamilton* (London: Tamesis, 1976), 195-214

Many of the recent collections of ballads from the modern oral tradition include musical transcriptions, and in several instances are accompanied by cassette recordings.

I

HISTORICAL BALLADS

KING RODERICK, LAST OF THE GOTHS

The ballads about King Roderick and the conquest of Spain by the Muslims in 711-13 are exceptional in the *Romancero* in that they are quite clearly based on a newly-composed, non-traditional chronicle. This was Pedro del Corral's *Corónica sarracina* composed in about 1430. If we were to view this as a historical text we might agree with Pérez de Guzmán, who in 1455 called it 'trufa o mentira palatina' and said it should be banned; but if we look at it as a historical novel we can easily see why it so attracted the poets of the day and led them to turn several of its episodes into ballads. Corral was a gifted writer who gave a definitive and highly-coloured version of legends which had been elaborated over the centuries among the various parties who gained or suffered from the invasion: the Muslims, the Gothic refugees of Asturias, the Christian masses who stayed on their lands under Muslim rule ('*Mozárabes*'), and the nobles and churchmen among them.

Exactly how the invasion of 711 took place is not known. The Muslims had completed the conquest of Morocco in 710 and would in any case have been tempted to invade the pleasant land they could see across the water. In the event, they were aided by a dynastic dispute within the Gothic state of Spain, in which the new king Roderick was opposed by the sons of Witiza, the previous ruler, and by others of his party, such as Bishop Oppa of Seville; and the Muslims found allies among the disaffected Jews of the kingdom who had suffered persecution. The invasion seems to have been carried out with surprising ease; within a few years the Peninsula was subdued and the Muslim armies were pressing well to the north of the Pyrenees.

The popular imagination and the bitterness of the defeated do not allow such momentous happenings to go unembroidered in the memory. The disaster must be seen in terms of persons and passions, and it must be moralised. If God allowed the Christians to be defeated it must be because of their sins of lust, thirst for vengeance, and treachery. So the legends began: a multiplicity of legends, agreed on a few central facts. It was said

1

that Count Julián (or Olbán, Yllán, Olián, etc.), Visigothic governor of Ceuta on the Moroccan coast, sent his daughter to be educated at the court of King Roderick at Toledo. There the King seduced her, and the girl sent word of it to her father. Julián, to secure his personal revenge, enlisted the aid of the Muslim generals in Morocco and encompassed the destruction not only of Roderick but of the whole state, handing a substantial part of Christendom to the infidel. Such is the essence of the legend which 'explained' a great defeat, just as the *Chanson de Roland* and the *Battle of Maldon* explained and also gloried in defeats in the following centuries.

The three ballads here printed were no doubt the work of rather more cultured poets than was usual, as is shown by their general tone, by the allegorical figure of *Fortuna*, and by somewhat untypical features in the King's lament. But they were early enough to become fully traditional. Other ballads describe the portents of the disaster, the affair between the King and Julián's daughter (her name, La Cava, Alacaba, apparently comes from the Arabic word for 'whore'), and the penance imposed upon the King for his sin.

On the legend, see R. Menéndez Pidal, *El rey Rodrigo en la literatura española* (Madrid: La Lectura, 1924), and *Floresta de leyendas heroicas españolas. Rodrigo, el último godo,* 3 vols (Madrid: La Lectura, 1925-7) (Clásicos Castellanos Nos. 62, 71, 84, including Pedro del Corral's text). On the ballads, see *Rom. trad.* I, 3-139; *Tratado*, I, 133-75; Wright, *CG*, 18-19.

1

En Ceuta está don Julián
en Ceuta la bien nombrada:
para las partes de allende
quiere enviar su embajada:
moro viejo la escribía,   5
y el conde se la notaba;
después de haberla escrito
al moro luego matara.
Embajada es de dolor,
dolor para toda España: 10
las cartas van al rey moro
en las cuales le juraba
que si le daba aparejo
le dará por suya España.
    Madre España, ¡ay de ti!   15
en el mundo tan nombrada,
de las partidas la mejor,
la mejor y más ufana,

donde nace el oro fino
y la plata no faltaba,   20
dotada de hermosura
y en proezas extremada;
por un perverso traidor
toda eres abrasada,
todas tus ricas ciudades   25
* con su gente tan galana
las domeñan hoy los moros
por nuestra culpa malvada,
si no fueran las Asturias
por ser la tierra tan brava.   30
   El triste rey don Rodrigo,
el que entonces te mandaba,
viendo sus reinos perdidos
sale a la campal batalla,
el cual en grave dolor   35
enseña su fuerza brava;
mas tantos eran los moros
que han vencido la batalla.
No parece el rey Rodrigo,
ni nadie sabe dó estaba.   40
Maldito de ti, don Orpas,
obispo de mala andanza:
en esta negra conseja
uno a otro se ayudaba.
¡Oh dolor sobre manera!   45
¡Oh cosa nunca cuidada!
que por sola una doncella
la cual Cava se llamaba
causen estos dos traidores
que España sea domeñada,   50
y perdido el rey señor
sin nunca dél saber nada.

TEXT: *Prim.* No. 4, from *Canc. de Rom.* of 1550.

TRANSLATION: Wright No. 28.

REFERENCES: *Rom. trad.* I, 35-40; Wright, *CG*, 19-20.

NOTES: This ballad derives as much from the *Estoria de España* as from Pedro del Corral. In parts it is popular enough, but traces of the *juglaresco* manner survive (e.g. 'la cual Cava se llamaba'). The section beginning 'Madre España...' is a memory of a fine piece of rhetoric in praise of Spain, the *Loor de España*, which through the *Estoria de España* and the *Poema de Fernán González* of the later 13th century ultimately derives from St Isidore (560-636). The ballad is known in the modern oral tradition from a single Portuguese version from the Algarve.

2

Los vientos eran contrarios,
la luna estaba crecida,
los peces daban gemidos
por el mal tiempo que hacia,
cuando el rey don Rodrigo   5
junto a la Cava dormía,
dentro de una rica tienda
de oro bien guarnecida.
Trescientas cuerdas de plata
que la tienda sostenían,   10
dentro había doncellas
vestidas a maravilla;
las cincuenta están tañendo
con muy extraña armonía,
las cincuenta están cantando   15
con muy dulce melodía.
    Allí hablara una doncella
que Fortuna se decía:
'Si duermes, rey don Rodrigo,
despierta por cortesía,   20
y verás tus malos hados,
tu peor postrimería,
y verás tus gentes muertas
y tu batalla rompida,
y tus villas y ciudades   25
destruidas en un día:
tus castillos, fortalezas,
otro señor los regía.
Si me pides quién lo ha hecho
yo muy bien te lo diría: 30
ese conde don Julián
por amores de su hija,
porque se la deshonraste
y más de ella no tenía.
Juramento viene echando   35
que te ha de costar la vida.'

4

Despertó muy congojado
con aquella voz que oía;
con cara triste y penosa
de esta suerte respondía: 40
'Mercedes a ti, Fortuna,
de esta tu mensajería.'
    Estando en esto allegó
uno que nuevas traía:
como el conde don Julián   45
las tierras le destruía.

TEXT: *Prim.* No. 5a, from Timoneda's *Rosa española* of 1573.

TRANSLATION: Gibson p. 281.

REFERENCES: *Tratado* I, 170; *Rom. trad.* I, 42-7; Wright, *CG*, 20.

NOTES: This is probably the oldest of the King Roderick ballads, com-
posed in the second half of the 15th century and soon so well-known that
in 1512 it was imitated in a ballad about the King of Navarre's loss of his
kingdom. Timoneda's text has here been shorn of its last 8 lines, in
accordance with Lapesa's suggestion that the ballad in its traditional form
really stopped at this point. In the oral tradition of Asturias, a few lines
from the start survive as the beginning of a ballad on a Nativity theme.

3

Las huestes de don Rodrigo
desmayaban y huían
cuando en la octava batalla
sus enemigos vencían.
Rodrigo deja sus tiendas   5
y del real se salía;
solo va el desventurado
que no lleva compañía.
El caballo de cansado
ya mudar no se podía;   10
camina por donde quiere
que no le estorba la vía.
El rey va tan desmayado
que sentido no tenía;
muerto va de sed y hambre   15
que de verle era mancilla,
iba tan tinto de sangre
que una brasa parecía.

Las armas lleva abolladas
que eran de gran pedrería;   20
la espada lleva hecha sierra
de los golpes que tenía;
el almete abollado
en la cabeza se le hundía;
la cara lleva hinchada   25
del trabajo que sufría.
Subióse encima de un cerro
el más alto que veía:
desde allí mira su gente
cómo iba de vencida;   30
de allí mira sus banderas
y estandartes que tenía,
cómo están todos pisados
que la tierra los cubría.
Mira por sus capitanes   35
que ninguno parecía;
mira el campo tinto en sangre
la cual arroyos corría.
El triste, de ver aquesto,
gran mancilla en sí tenía: 40
llorando de los sus ojos
de esta manera decía:
    'Ayer era rey de España,
hoy no lo soy de una villa;
ayer villas y castillos,   45
hoy ninguno poseía;
ayer tenía criados,
hoy ninguno me servía;
hoy no tengo una almena
que pueda decir que es mía.   50
¡Desdichada fue la hora
desdichado fue aquel día
en que nací y heredé
la tan grande señoría,
pues lo había de perder   55
todo junto y en un día!
¡Oh muerte! ¿Por qué no vienes
y llevas esta alma mía
de aqueste cuerpo mezquino
pues se te agradecería?'   60

TEXT: *Prim.* No. 5, from *Canc. de Rom. 'sin año'* (c. 1548).

TRANSLATIONS: Lockhart No. 1, 'The Lamentation of Don Roderick'; Gibson p. 282; Wright No. 29; and in French, Victor Hugo under the title of 'La Bataille perdue', No. XVI of *Les Orientales*.

REFERENCES: *Tratado* I, 168; *Rom. trad.* I, 47-53.

NOTES: Numerous references to this ballad and imitations of it show how much the poem was esteemed during the Golden Age. Lope de Vega glossed it in his play *El último godo*, and Cervantes has Maese Pedro quote a part of it after the destruction of his puppet-kingdom by Don Quixote (II, 26). It is said that the ballad was sung by a minstrel to King Sebastião of Portugal aboard the ship carrying the expedition to Morocco in 1578; when the line 'Ayer era rey de España' was reached it was taken as an omen, and a courtier ordered the minstrel to sing something more cheerful. (Sebastião and most of his army perished at Alcazarquivir a few weeks later.) The ballad survived in the oral tradition of Galicia about 1900. For the multitude of plays, novels, and poems which have retold the legend of Roderick, see Menéndez Pidal's books *El rey Rodrigo* and vol. 3 of the *Floresta*.

BERNARDO DEL CARPIO

The Bernardo ballads derive from a lost epic and from legends incorporated in rather diverse forms in the chronicles. Both epic and legends were no more than pseudo-historical. They sprang up in the late 12th and 13th centuries as a nationalistic answer to the extravagant claims made in French chronicles and in the opening lines of the *Chanson de Roland* (then becoming known in Spain) to the effect that Charlemagne and his Franks had liberated most of the Peninsula from the Moors. The Spaniards adapted a legend about Charlemagne's sister Berthe, and had Bernardo defeat Roland and the Twelve Peers at Roncesvaux. Of greater human interest and dramatic potentiality, however, was that part of the legend which concerned Bernardo's birth, the imprisonment of his father, and Bernardo's efforts to secure his father's release, a typical king-and-vassal situation with a fine tragic ending.

The legend is Leonese rather than Castilian: Carpio is a castle on the Tormes near Salamanca, in Leonese lands, and Alfonso II 'el Casto' ruled Leon from 791 to 835.

Of the three ballads, only No. 6 is a true epic fragment. The other two, in less lively narrative style, were composed in the 16th century on the basis of chronicle accounts.

On the legend, epic, and ballads, see *Tratado* I, 176-216; W.J. Entwistle, 'The *Cantar de gesta* of Bernardo del Carpio', *Modern Language Review* 23 (1928) 307-22 and 432-52; *Rom. trad.* I, 143-270; Wright, *CG*, 23-5.

4

En los reinos de León
el casto Alfonso reinaba;
hermosa hermana tenía
doña Jimena se llama.
Enamorárase de ella   5
ese conde de Saldaña,
mas no vivía engañado
porque la infanta lo amaba.
Muchas veces fueron juntos
que nadie lo sospechaba;   10
de las veces que se vieron
la infanta quedó preñada.
La infanta parió a Bernaldo
y luego monja se entraba;
mandó el rey prender al conde   15
y ponerle muy gran guarda.

TEXT: *Prim.* No. 8, from *Canc. de Rom.* of 1550.

TRANSLATION: Wright No. 23.

REFERENCES: *Rom. trad.* I, 176-84; Wright, *CG*, 25.

NOTES: This is an example of a wholly narrative ballad which manages to tell in concise form the main facts upon which the legend and cycle of ballads is based. A number of versions of it, in much extended form and with accretions from other cycles, have been recorded among the Sephardic Jews of Morocco.

5

Por las riberas de Arlanza
Bernardo del Carpio cabalga,
con un caballo morcillo
enjaezado de grana,
gruesa lanza en la mano,   5
armado de todas armas.
Toda la gente de Burgos
le mira como espantada,
porque no se suele armar
sino a cosa señalada.   10
También lo miraba el rey
que fuera a vuela una garza;
diciendo estaba a los suyos:

'Esta es una buena lanza;
si no es Bernardo del Carpio   15
éste es Muza el de Granada.'
    Ellos estando en aquesto
Bernardo que allí llegaba:
ya sosegado el caballo
no quiso dejar la lanza;   20
mas puesta encima del hombro
al rey de esta suerte hablaba:
'Bastardo me llaman, rey,
siendo hijo de tu hermana
y del noble Sancho Díaz   25
ese conde de Saldaña;
dicen que ha sido traidor
y mala mujer tu hermana.
Tu y los tuyos lo habéis dicho,
que otro ninguno no osara;   30
mas quien quiera que lo ha dicho
miente por medio la barba;
mi padre no fue traidor
ni mi madre mujer mala,
porque cuando fui engendrado   35
ya mi madre era casada.
Pusiste a mi padre en hierros
y a mi madre en orden santa,
y porque no herede yo
quieres dar tu reino a Francia.   40
Morirán los castellanos
antes de ver tal jornada;
montañeses, y leoneses,
y esa gente asturiana,
y ese rey de Zaragoza   45
me prestará su compaña
para salir contra Francia
y darle cruda batalla;
y si buena me saliere
será el bien de toda España;   50
si mala, por la república
moriré yo en tal demanda.
Mi padre mando que sueltes
pues me diste la palabra;
si no, en campo, como quiera,   55
te será bien demandada.'

9

TEXT: *Prim.* No. 12, from Timoneda's *Rosa española* of 1573.

TRANSLATION: Wright No. 35.

REFERENCE: *Rom. trad.* I, 184-91.

NOTES: This ballad was newly composed in the mid-16th century and was soon recorded in a number of differing versions, showing a certain popularity. The anonymous author has very successfully caught the 'brío' of the older ballads, but his geography was shaky (Burgos stands on the Arlanzón, not the Arlanza). The ballad is glossed by Lope de Vega in his play *Las mocedades de Bernardo del Carpio.*

6

Con cartas y mensajeros
el rey al Carpio envió:
Bernaldo, como es discreto,
de traición se receló;
las cartas echó en el suelo 5
y al mensajero habló:
'Mensajero eres, amigo,
no mereces culpa, no;
mas al rey que acá te envía
dígasle tú esta razón: 10
que no lo estimo yo a él
ni aun a cuantos con él son;
mas, por ver lo que me quiere,
todavía allá iré yo.'
Y mandó juntar los suyos, 15
de esta suerte les habló:
'Cuatrocientos sois, los míos,
los que comedes mi pan:
los ciento irán al Carpio
para el castillo guardar; 20
los ciento por los caminos
que a nadie dejen pasar;
doscientos iréis conmigo
para con el rey hablar;
si mala me la dijere 25
peor se le he de tornar.'
Por sus jornadas contadas
a la corte fue a llegar:
'Manténgavos Dios, buen rey,
y a cuantos con vos están.' 30

10

'Mal vengades vos, Bernaldo,
traidor, hijo de mal padre;
dite yo el Carpio en tenencia,
tú tómaslo de heredad.'
'Mentides, el rey, mentides,   35
que no dices la verdad;
que si yo fuese traidor
a vos os cabría en parte:
acordársevos debía
de aquella del Encinal,   40
cuando gentes extranjeras
allí os trataron tan mal,
que os mataron el caballo
y aun a vos querían matar:
Bernaldo, como traidor,   45
de entre ellos os fue a sacar,
allí me distes el Carpio
de juro y de heredad;
prometístesme a mi padre,
no me guardastes verdad.'   50
'¡Prendedlo, mis caballeros,
que igualado se me ha!'
'¡Aquí, aquí, los mis doscientos,
los que comedes mi pan,
que hoy era venido el día   55
que honra habemos de ganar!'
El rey, de que aquesto viera,
de esta suerte fue a hablar:
'¿Qué ha sido aquesto, Bernaldo,
que así enojado te has?   60
¿Lo que hombre dice de burla
de veras vas a tomar?
Yo te do el Carpio, Bernaldo,
de juro y de heredad.'
'Aquesas burlas, el rey,   65
no son burlas de burlar;
llamástesme de traidor
traidor hijo de mal padre;
el Carpio yo no lo quiero,
bien lo podéis vos guardar,   70
que cuando yo lo quisiere
muy bien lo sabré ganar.'

11

TEXT: *Prim.* No. 36.

REFERENCES: *Rom. trad.* I, 155-75; Wright, *CG*, 25-8.

NOTES: Although Entwistle thought the ballad contaminated with *Castellanos y leoneses* (No. 8) about the interview between Fernán González and the king, the Spanish scholars are agreed that in its lively style and its change of assonance this is a genuine fragment of the epic of Bernardo. It was well known in the 16th century, and oral versions have been collected in Cadiz and Seville.

FERNAN GONZALEZ

When Castile is first heard of in history, it is as a county subject to the monarchs of Asturias-Leon. Its independence was won for it in the mid-10th century by Count Fernán González, about whose noble memory it was natural that legend should gather. On the legends a monk of San Pedro de Arlanza based his *Poema de Fernán González* (c. 1270), giving them a notably pious character, and this *clerecía* work was prosified in the *Estoria de España* a few years later. But there existed also an epic *cantar* which has left substantial traces of itself in the prose of the *Crónica de 1344*, and from which there derive the ballads here printed. Of these the first (No. 7) is the most remote from the epic tradition, but the other two are typical epic scenes narrated with proper vigour.

The ballads of Fernán González told for preference not of the independence of Castile, nor of his battles against Almanzor, but of his disputes with the kings of Leon and Navarre. In No. 7 the Count wins his second wife, Sancha of Navarre.

On the legends and the ballads, see *Tratado* I, 217-64; D. Catalán & others, *Rom. trad.* II, 1-81; René Cotrait, *Histoire et poésie: Le Comte Fernán González* (Grenoble: Allier, 1977); Wright, *CG*, 26-8. The *Poema de Fernán González* has several modern editions, among them that by Juan Victorio (Madrid: Cátedra, 1981).

7

Preso está Fernán González
el gran conde de Castilla,
tiénelo el rey de Navarra
maltratado a maravilla.
Vino allí un conde normando   5
que pasaba en romería;
supo que este hombre famoso
en cárceles padecía.

Fuese para Castroviejo
donde el conde residía;   10
dádivas daba al alcaide
si dejar verle quería;
el alcaide fue contento
y las prisiones le abría.
Mucho los condes hablaron;   15
el normando se salía;
fuese donde estaba el rey
con lo que pensado había.
Procuró ver a la infanta
que era hermosa y cumplida,   20
animosa y muy discreta,
de persona muy crecida.
Tanto procura de verla
que esto le hablara un día:
    'Dios vos lo perdone, infanta,   25
Dios, también Santa María,
que por vos se pierde un hombre
el mejor que se sabía;
por vos se causa gran daño,
por vos se pierde Castilla: 30
los moros entran en ella,
por no ver quien la regía,
que por veros muere preso
por amor de vos moría:
¡mal pagáis amor, infanta,   35
a quien tanto en vos confía!
Si no remediáis al conde
seréis muy aborrecida,
y si por vos saliese
seréis reina de Castilla.'   40
    Tan bien le habla el normando
que a la infanta enternecía:
determina de librarlo
si por mujer la quería.
El conde se lo promete,   45
a verlo la infanta iba:
'No temáis', dijo, 'señor,
que yo os daré la salida.'
    Y engañando aquel alcaide
salen los dos de la villa.   50
Toda la noche anduvieron

hasta que el alba reía.
Escondidos en un bosque
un arcipreste los veía
que venía andando a caza   55
con un azor que traía.
Amenázalos con muerte
si la infanta no ofrecía
de folgar allí con ella,
si no, que al rey los traería.   60
El conde más cruda muerte
quisiera, que lo que oía;
pero la discreta infanta
dando esfuerzo, le decía:
'Por vuestra vida, señor,   65
más que esto hacer debría,
que no se sabrá esta afrenta
ni se dirá en esta vida.'
    Prisa daba el arcipreste,
y amenaza todavía;   70
con grillos estaba el conde
y sin armas se veía;
mas viendo que era forzado
como puede se desvía.
Apártala el arcipreste,   75
de la mano la traía,
y cuando abrazarla quiso
ella de él muy fuerte huía;
los brazos le ha embarazado,
socorro al conde pedía,   80
el cual vino apresurado
aunque correr no podía:
quitádole ha al arcipreste
un cuchillo que traía,
y con él le diera el pago   85
que su aleve merecía.
    Ayudándole la infanta
camina todo aquel día;
a la bajada de un puente
ven muy gran caballería;   90
gran miedo tienen en verla
porque creen que el rey la envía.
La infanta tiembla y se muere,
en el monte se escondía;

mas el conde, más mirando,   95
daba voces de alegría:
'Salid, salid, doña Sancha,
ved el pendón de Castilla,
míos son los caballeros
que a mi socorro venían.'   100
La infanta con gran placer
a verlos luego salía;
conocidos de los suyos
con alarido venían:
'¡Castilla!' vienen diciendo,   105
'cumplida es la jura hoy día.'
A los dos besan la mano,
a caballo los subían,
así los traen en salvo
al condado de Castilla.   110

TEXT: *Prim.* No. 15, from *Canc. de Rom.* of 1550.

TRANSLATION: Lockhart No. 8, 'The Escape of Count Fernan Gonsalez'.

NOTES: Compare *Poema de Fernán González*, stanzas 597-681.

8

Castellanos y leoneses
tienen grandes divisiones:
el conde Fernán González
y el buen rey Sancho Ordóñez,
sobre el partir de las tierras   5
y el poner de los mojones;
llamábanse hideputas,
hijos de padres traidores;
echan mano a las espadas,
derriban ricos mantones;   10
no les pueden poner treguas
cuantos en la corte son,
pónenselas dos hermanos
aquesos benditos monjes.
Pónenlas por quince días   15
que no pueden por más, no,
que se vayan a los prados
que dicen de Carrión.
Si mucho madruga el rey
el conde no dormía, no;   20

el conde partió de Burgos,
y el rey partió de León.
Venido se han a juntar
al vado de Carrión,
y a la pasada del río   25
movieron una cuestión:
los del rey que pasarían,
y los del conde que no.
El rey, como era risueño,
la su mula revolvió;   30
el conde con lozanía
su caballo arremetió;
con el agua y la arena
al buen rey ensalpicó.
    Allí hablara el buen rey,   35
su gesto muy demudado:
'¡Cómo sois soberbio, el conde!
¡cómo sois desmesurado!
si no fuera por las treguas
que los monjes nos han dado,   40
la cabeza de los hombros
ya vos la hubiera quitado;
con la sangre que os sacara
yo tiñera aqueste vado.'
    El conde le respondiera   45
como aquél que era osado:
'Eso que decís, buen rey,
véolo mal aliñado;
vos venís en gruesa mula,
yo en ligero caballo;   50
vos traéis sayo de seda,
yo traigo un arnés tranzado;
vos traéis alfanje de oro,
yo traigo lanza en mi mano;
vos traéis cetro de rey,   55
yo un venablo acerado;
vos con guantes olorosos,
yo con los de acero claro;
vos con la gorra de fiesta,
yo con un casco afinado;   60
vos traéis ciento de mula,
yo trescientos de caballo.'

Ellos en aquesto estando
los frailes que han allegado:
'¡Tate, tate, caballeros!   65
¡Tate, tate, hijosdalgo!
¡Cuán mal cumplistes las treguas
que nos habíades mandado!'
Allí hablara el buen rey:
'Yo las cumpliré de grado.'   70
Pero respondiera el conde:
'Yo de pies puesto en el campo.'
Cuando vido aquesto el rey
no quiso pasar el vado;
vuélvese para sus tierras,   75
malamente va enojado.
Grandes bascas va haciendo,
reciamente va jurando
que había de matar al conde
y destruir su condado,   80
y mandó llamar a cortes,
por los grandes ha enviado;
todos ellos son venidos,
sólo el conde ha faltado.
Mensajero se le hace   85
a que cumpla su mandado;
el mensajero que fue
de esta suerte le ha hablado:...

TEXT: *Prim.* No. 16, from *Silva de varios romances* of 1550.

NOTES: It is typical of the ballad spirit that the reader is clearly expected
to take the side of Fernán González against the King, even though the text
frankly states that the Count was in the wrong in the incident at the ford.
The contrasts between Fernán González, disrespectful to King, friars, and
truce, but every inch a figure of epic stature, and the effete King, are well
brought out in the antithetical lines and were much to the taste of the 16th
century. The ballad is meant to continue into the next:

9

'Buen conde Fernán González
el rey envía por vos,
que vayades a las cortes
que se hacían en León;
que si vos allá vais, conde,   5
daros han buen galardón:

daros han a Palenzuela
y a Palencia la mayor;
daros han las nueve villas
con ellas a Carrión;   10
daros han a Torquemada,
la torre de Mormojón.
Buen conde, si allá no ides,
daros han por traidor.'
   Allí respondiera el conde   15
y dijera esta razón:
'Mensajero eres, amigo,
no mereces culpa, no;
que yo no he miedo al rey
ni a cuantos con él son.   20
Villas y castillos tengo,
todos a mi mandar son;
de ellos me dejó mi padre,
de ellos me ganara yo;
los que me dejó mi padre   25
poblélos de ricos hombres,
los que yo me hube ganado
poblélos de labradores;
quien no tenía más de un buey
dábale otro, que eran dos;   30
al que casaba su hija
dóle yo muy rico don;
cada día que amanece
por mí hacen oración;
no la hacían por el rey,   35
que no la merece, no;
él les puso muchos pechos
y quitáraselos yo.'

TEXT: *Prim*. No. 17, from *Silva de varios romances* of 1550.

NOTES: It will be observed that lines very similar to lines 17-20 have already appeared in a Bernardo del Carpio ballad (No. 6). This is a typical contamination, and it is impossible to determine which ballad had priority. The naming of Palencia with an epic epithet, 'la mayor', we can however affirm to be a borrowing from the *Poema de mio Cid*, in which we find 'Valencia la mayor' eight times (e.g., line 2105), though Armistead thinks it simply 'an independent occurrence of the same formulaic epithet'.

THE SIETE INFANTES DE LARA

The epic of the *Siete Infantes* does not survive as a poetic text, but portions of it have been reconstructed as verse from the prosified versions which were written into the chronicles (e.g. of 1344 and c. 1460). From late versions of the epic the following four ballads derive in different ways. The extraordinary tale of the *Siete Infantes* is based upon what may have been events of the late 10th century, when Count Garci-Fernández (son of Fernán González) ruled in Castile and the great Al-Mansur, Almanzor, was virtual dictator of Muslim Spain on behalf of the Caliph Hisham II. Some maintain that an early epic was composed shortly following these events, but there is no evidence for its existence before the 13th century and the poem is probably a creation of that time, perhaps based on a tradition preserved in the great family of the Laras. The four ballads contain the essential narration of the whole epic: the marriage between members of two powerful families, the insult at the wedding of doña Lambra, the bloody vengeance taken by the bridegroom don Rodrigo de Lara on his seven nephews, the lament of their father (a prisoner in Cordova) over their severed heads, and the final vengeance of Mudarra. The tale of insult, feud, treachery, and vengeance seems to preserve features of a remote Spanish past in which Germanic customs hold sway and Christian restraints are absent; but evidently later periods still much enjoyed their blood-and-thunder dramas.

On the legend and the ballads, see R. Menéndez Pidal, *La leyenda de los Infantes de Lara*, 3rd ed. (Madrid: Espasa-Calpe, 1971); *Tratado* I, 265-89; *Rom. trad.* II, 85-252; Wright, *CG*, 28-9. The relevant chronicle texts and reconstructed portions of the epic are in Menéndez Pidal's *Reliquias de la poesía épica española*, 2nd ed. (Madrid: Gredos, 1980), 181-239. As a curiosity for British readers, see Colin Smith, 'The "Siete Infantes" Reborn in Scotland', *La Corónica* 18 (1989-90) 83-90.

10

A Calatrava la Vieja
la combaten castellanos;
por cima de Guadiana
derribaron tres pedazos:
por los dos salen los moros,   5
por el uno entran cristianos.
Allá dentro de la plaza
fueron a armar un tablado,
que aquel que lo derribare
ganará de oro un escaño.   10

Este don Rodrigo de Lara
– que ése lo había ganado –
del conde Garcí-Hernández sobrino
y de doña Sancha es hermano,
al conde Garcí-Hernández   15
se lo llevó presentado,
que le trate casamiento
con aquesa doña Lambra.
　　Ya se trata casamiento,
¡hecho fue en hora menguada!   20
doña Lambra de Burueva
con don Rodrigo de Lara.
Las bodas fueron en Burgos,
las tornabodas en Salas;
en bodas y tornabodas   25
pasaron siete semanas.
Tantas vienen de las gentes
que no caben por las plazas,
y aún faltaban por venir
los siete infantes de Lara.   30
　　¡Hélos, hélos por do vienen
con toda la su compaña!
saliólos a recibir
la su madre doña Sancha:
'Bien vengades, los mis hijos,   35
buena sea vuestra llegada:
allá iredes a posar
a esa cal de Cantarranas;
hallaréis las mesas puestas,
viandas aparejadas.   40
Desque hayáis comido, hijos,
no salgades a las plazas,
porque las gentes son muchas,
y trábanse muchas barajas.'
　　Desque todos han comido   45
van a bohordar a la plaza;
no salen los siete infantes,
que su madre se lo mandara;
mas desque hubieron comido
siéntanse a jugar las tablas.   50
　　Tiran unos, tiran otros,
ninguno bien bohordaba.
Allí salió un caballero

de los de Córdoba la llana,
bohordó hacia el tablado   55
y una vara bien tirara.
Allí habló la novia,
de esta manera hablara:
'Amad, señoras, amad
cada una en su lugar,   60
que más vale un caballero
de los de Córdoba la llana,
que no veinte ni treinta
de los de la casa de Lara.'
Oídolo había doña Sancha,   65
de esta manera hablara:
'No digáis eso, señora,
no digades tal palabra,
porque aun hoy os desposaron
con don Rodrigo de Lara.'   70
'Mas calléis vos, doña Sancha,
que no debéis ser escuchada,
que siete hijos paristes
como puerca encenagada.'
        Oídolo había el ayo   75
que a los infantes criaba;
de allí se había salido,
triste se fue a su posada;
halló que estaban jugando
los infantes a las tablas,   80
si no era el menor de ellos,
Gonzalo González se llama;
recostado lo halló
de pechos en una baranda:
'¿Cómo venís triste, ayo?   85
decid, ¿quién os enojara?'
Tanto le rogó Gonzalo
que el ayo se lo contara:
'Mas mucho os ruego, mi hijo,
que no salgáis a la plaza.'   90
No lo quiso hacer Gonzalo,
mas antes tomó una lanza,
caballero en un caballo
váse derecho a la plaza:
vido estar el tablado   95
que nadie lo derribara.

21

Enderezóse en la silla,
con él en el suelo daba;
desque lo hubo derribado
de esta manera hablara: 100
'Amade, putas, amad,
cada una en su lugar,
que más vale un caballero
de los de la casa de Lara
que cuarenta ni cincuenta   105
de los de Córdoba la llana.'
    Doña Lambra, que esto oyera,
bajóse muy enojada;
sin aguardar a los suyos
fuese para su posada,   110
halló en ella a don Rodrigo,
de esta manera le habla:
'Yo me estaba en Barbadillo
en esa mi heredad;
mal me quieren en Castilla   115
los que me habían de aguardar.
Los hijos de doña Sancha
mal amenazado me han
que me cortarían las faldas
por vergonzoso lugar,   120
y cebarían sus halcones
dentro de mi palomar,
y me forzarían mis damas
casadas y por casar.
Matáronme un cocinero   125
so faldas de mi brial.
Si de esto no me vengáis
yo mora me iré a tornar.'
    Allí habló don Rodrigo,
bien oiréis lo que dirá: 130
'Calledes, la mi señora,
vos no digades atal.
De los infantes de Lara
yo vos pienso de vengar;
telilla les tengo urdida,   135
bien se la cuido tramar,
que nacidos y por nacer
de ello tengan que contar.'

TEXT: *Prim.* No. 19, from *Canc. de Rom. 'sin año'* (c. 1548).

REFERENCES: *Rom. hisp.* I, 205-6, and II, 75-6.

NOTES: This magnificent ballad derives directly from the epic, but it is a summary of a series of fragments rather than a single passage of the original. The mentions of Calatrava la Vieja and Cordova are the result of some contamination, since in the 10th century both lay well outside Christian territory: Calatrava (a famous fortress in the province of Ciudad Real) was not conquered until 1147, was later lost again, and not finally taken until 1212, while Cordova (the capital of the Caliphs) was not taken until 1236. This illustrates how little geographical exactness matters to the ballad; names are used for their romantic and heroic appeal and their sound. Doña Lambra's name derives, fittingly for her passionate nature, from *Flammula* ('Little Flame'). The ballad was already popular enough to be parodied in 1475, and was famous during the 16th century.

11

Saliendo de Canicosa
por el val de Arabiana,
donde don Rodrigo espera
los hijos de la su hermana,
por campo de Palomares   5
vio venir muy gran compaña,
muchas armas reluciendo,
mucha adarga bien labrada,
mucho caballo ligero,
mucha lanza relumbraba,   10
mucho estandarte y bandera
por los aires revolaba.
La seña que viene en ellas
es media luna cortada;
Alá traen por apellido,   15
A Mahoma a voces llaman;
tan altos daban los gritos
que los campos resonaban;
lo que las voces decían
grande mal significaba: 20
'¡Mueran, mueran', van diciendo,
'los siete infantes de Lara!
¡Venguemos a don Rodrigo
pues que tiene de ellos saña!'
Allí está Nuño Salido,   25

el ayo que los criara;
como ve la gran morisma
de esta manera les habla:
'¡Oh los mis amados hijos!
¡Quién vivo no se hallara   30
por no ver tan gran dolor
como agora se esperaba!
Si no os hubiera criado
no sintiera tanta rabia;
mas quiéroos tanto, mis hijos,   35
que se me arrancaba el alma.
¡Ciertamente nuestra muerte
está bien aparejada!
No podemos escapar
de tanta gente pagana.   40
Vendamos bien nuestros cuerpos
y miremos por las almas:
peleemos como buenos,
las muertes queden vengadas;
ya que lleven nuestras vidas   45
que las dejen bien pagadas.
No nos pese de la muerte,
pues va tan bien empleada,
pues morimos todos juntos
como buenos, en batalla.'   50
    Como los moros se acercan
a cada uno por sí abraza;
cuando llega a Gonzalvico
en la cara le besara:
'¡Hijo Gonzalo González!   55
de lo que más me pesaba
es de lo que sentirá
vuestra madre doña Sancha.
Erades su claro espejo,
más que a todos os amaba.'   60
    En esto los moros llegan,
traban con ellos batalla,
los infantes los reciben
con sus adargas y lanzas.
'¡Santiago, Santiago!'   65
a grandes voces llamaban;
matan infinitos moros
mas todos allí quedaran.

TEXT: *Prim.* No. 23, from *Silva de varios romances* of 1550.

NOTES: Le Strange, following Milá, notes that the reference to 'media luna' and the distinction drawn between Allah and Muhammad mark this ballad as a rather late one. Menéndez Pidal confirms this, stating that it is based on the chronicles rather than the epic, and is to be dated to c. 1540. None the less, the author successfully imitated much of the style of the true *romances viejos*. Canicosa does exist, in the ancient territory of Lara or Salas (Salas de los Infantes lies some 50 km to the south-east of Burgos). Palomares and Arabiana are probably inventions of the poet. Le Strange remarks that 'a hill, two leagues from Córdoba, is still shown by the people as the place where the Infantes de Lara were slain'.

12

> Pártese el moro Alicante
> víspera de San Cebrián;
> ocho cabezas llevaba
> todos de hombres de alta sangre.
> Sábelo el rey Almanzor,   5
> a recibírselo sale;
> aunque perdió muchos moros
> piensa en esto bien ganar.
> Manda hacer un tablado
> para mejor las mirar,   10
> mandó traer un cristiano
> que estaba en cautividad.
> Como ante sí lo trajeron
> empezóle de hablar,
> díjole: 'Gonzalo Gustos,   15
> mira quién conocerás:
> que lidiaron mis poderes
> en el campo de Almenar;
> sacaron ocho cabezas,
> todos son de gran linaje.'   20
>   Respondió Gonzalo Gustos:
> 'Presto os diré la verdad.'
> Y limpiándoles de sangre
> asaz se fuera a turbar;
> dijo llorando agramente: 25
> '¡Conózcolas por mi mal!
> la una es de mi carillo;
> las otras me duelen más;
> de los infantes de Lara

son, mis hijos naturales.'   30
Así razona con ellos
como si vivos hablasen:
    '¡Dios os salve, el mi compadre,
el mi amigo leal!
¿Adónde son los mis hijos,   35
que yo os quise encomendar?
Muerto sois como buen hombre,
como hombre de fiar.'
    Tomara otra cabeza
del hijo mayor de edad: 40
'Sálveos Dios, Diego González,
hombre de muy gran bondad,
del conde Fernán González
alférez el principal;
a vos amaba yo mucho,   45
que me habíades de heredar.'
Alimpiándola con lágrimas
volviérala a su lugar.
    Y toma la del segundo,
Martín Gómez que llamaban: 50
'Dios os perdone, el mi hijo,
hijo que mucho preciaba;
jugador era de tablas
el mejor de toda España,
mesurado caballero,   55
muy buen hablador en plaza.'
    Y dejándola llorando
la del tercero tomaba:
'Hijo Suero Gustos,
todo el mundo os estimaba;   60
el rey os tuviera en mucho
sólo para la su caza;
gran caballero esforzado,
muy buen bracero a ventaja.
¡Ruy Gómez vuestro tío   65
estas bodas ordenara!'
    Y tomando la del cuarto
lasamente la miraba:
'¡Oh hijo Fernán González,
nombre del mejor de España,   70
del buen conde de Castilla
aquél que vos bautizara;

26

matador de puerco espín,
amigo de gran compaña!
Nunca con gente de poco   75
os vieran en alianza.'
   Tomó la de Ruy Gómez,
de corazón la abrazaba:
'¡Hijo mío, hijo mío!
¿Quién como vos se hallara?   80
nunca le oyeron mentira,
nunca por oro ni plata;
animoso, buen guerrero,
muy gran heridor de espada,
que a quien dábades de lleno   85
tullido o muerto quedaba.'
   Tomando la del menor
el dolor se le doblara:
'¡Hijo Gonzalo González!
¡Los ojos de doña Sancha!   90
¡Qué nuevas irán a ella
que a vos más que a todos ama!
Tan apuesto de persona,
decidor bueno entre damas,
repartidor en su haber,   95
aventajado en la lanza.
¡Mejor fuera la mi muerte
que ver tan triste jornada!'
   Al duelo que el viejo hace
toda Córdoba lloraba.   100
El rey Almanzor cuidoso
consigo se lo llevaba,
y mandó a una morica
lo sirviese muy de gana.
Esta le torna en prisiones   105
y con hambre le curaba.
Hermana era del rey,
doncella moza y lozana;
con ésta Gonzalo Gustos
vino a perder su saña,   110
que de ella le nació un hijo
que a los hermanos vengara.

TEXT: *Prim.* No. 24, from *Silva de varios romances* of 1550.

REFERENCES: *Tratado* I, 276-80; *Rom. hisp.* I, 203-5; J.G. Cummins, 'The Creative Process in the Ballad *Pártese el moro Alicante*', *Forum for Modern Language Studies* 6 (1970) 368-81.

NOTES: Le Strange follows Milá in drawing attention to the extraordinary confusion of personal names in this ballad. It may be that as with geographical names in other ballads, accuracy matters little; on the other hand, the patronymic system (González = son of Gonzalo) was well established and observed in the epic, which after all was about family and clan feelings. Menéndez Pidal gave special attention to this text, because in this case a direct comparison of ballad with parent epic is possible. The 112 short lines or 56 long lines of the ballad correspond to some 150 long lines of the epic text as prosified in the *Crónica de 1344*, and the ten assonance-series or laisses of the epic are reduced to two in the ballad.

The epic goes on to tell how Gonzalo Gustos is released and returns to Castile; his son (Mudarra) by the Moorish girl grows to manhood, learns of his parentage and goes to Castile to avenge his half-brothers:

13

A cazar va don Rodrigo,
y aun don Rodrigo de Lara,
con la gran siesta que hace
arrimádose ha a una haya,
maldiciendo a Mudarrillo   5
hijo de la renegada,
que si a las manos le hubiese
que le sacaría el alma.
El señor estando en esto,
Mudarrillo que asomaba: 10
'Dios te salve, caballero,
debajo la verde haya.'
'Así haga a ti, escudero,
buena sea tu llegada.'
'Dígasme tú, el caballero,   15
cómo era la tu gracia?'
'A mí dicen don Rodrigo,
y aun don Rodrigo de Lara,
cuñado de Gonzalo Gustos,
hermano de doña Sancha;   20
por sobrinos me los hube
los siete infantes de Lara.
Espero aquí a Mudarrillo,
hijo de la renegada:

si delante lo tuviese 25
yo le sacaría el alma.'
'Si a ti dicen don Rodrigo,
y aun don Rodrigo de Lara,
a mí Mudarra González,
hijo de la renegada, 30
de Gonzalo Gustos hijo,
y alnado de doña Sancha;
por hermanos me los hube
los siete infantes de Lara:
tú los vendiste, traidor, 35
en el val de Arabiana;
mas si Dios a mí ayuda
aquí dejarás el alma.'
'Espéresme, don Gonzalo,
iré a tomar las mis armas.' 40
'El espera que tú diste
a los infantes de Lara:
aquí morirás, traidor,
enemigo de doña Sancha.'

TEXT: *Prim.* No. 26, from *Canc. de Rom. 'sin año'* (c. 1548).

TRANSLATION: Lockhart No. 10, 'The Vengeance of Mudarra'; Gibson p. 287; and in French, Victor Hugo under the title of 'Romance Mauresque', No. XXX of *Les Orientales*.

REFERENCES: *Tratado* I, 280-4; *Rom. hisp.* I, 229-34; P. Bénichou, *Creación poética en el romancero tradicional* (Madrid: Gredos, 1968), 40-60.

NOTES: This ballad is based on a very late version of the epic. Whereas the previous ballad preserved a long and detailed narrative, this one is a fine example of the compression which is achieved as the text evolves. Menéndez Pidal calls it 'ejemplo extremo de novelización': all the armies and retainers and the geographical details of the epic have disappeared, and the two men confront each other alone. Two other 16th-century versions are known, and it is quoted in *Don Quixote* (II, 60); Lope de Vega used this and the previous ballads in his play *El bastardo Mudarra*.

KING SANCHO II AND THE SIEGE OF ZAMORA

By this name is known one of the lost epics of medieval Castile which, to judge from the versions prosified in the chronicles and from the ballads, was in its construction and its deep tragic sense as fine a work as the surviving *Poema de mio Cid*. The Zamora poem was, in fact, meant to accompany the *Poema de mio Cid*. The Cid appears prominently in it, and the last scene of the lost epic (or perhaps originally a separate poem) explains in part the bad feeling between King and Cid which is the basis for the opening scene of the *Poema*. The following seven ballads contain in essence the whole of the epic tale, which in general and in some of its details has a firm basis in history, though any part the Cid may have taken here in history was much enlarged in poetry.

King Ferdinand I of Leon-Castile lay dying in 1065, and then divided up his realm between his three sons, assigning (as something of an afterthought) Zamora to his daughter Urraca. Zamora was a fortress-town on the Duero, within Leonese lands. King Sancho of Castile in history defeated his brother Alfonso of Leon in 1072, and then besieged his sister in Zamora. The starving Zamorans, after rejecting the Cid's offer of negotiation, sent out Vellido Dolfos as a pretended deserter, and he treacherously killed King Sancho. The Castilians, seeing their monarch's death as a divine punishment upon him for having overset his father's will, raised the siege but held the city collectively responsible for the treachery (ballads 18 & 19). Finally Sancho's banished brother Alfonso returned from exile in Moorish Toledo to take the crowns of reunited Leon and Castile, but only after swearing in Burgos before the assembled Castilian nobles that he had had no part in Sancho's murder (ballad 20).

See *Tratado* I, 349-57; Carola Reig, *El Cantar de Sancho II y Cerco de Zamora* (Madrid: CSIC, 1947); Wright, *CG*, 29-36.

14

Doliente estaba, doliente,
ese buen rey don Fernando,
los pies tiene cara oriente
y la candela en la mano.
A la cabecera tiene   5
los sus hijos todos cuatro:
los tres eran de la reina,
y el uno era bastardo;
ése que bastardo era
quedaba mejor librado: 10
arzobispo es de Toledo
y en las Españas perlado.

'Si yo no muriera, hijo,
vos fuérades Padre Santo,
mas con la renta que os queda   15
bien podréis, hijo, alcanzarlo.'

TEXT: *Prim.* No. 35, from *Canc. de Rom. 'sin año'* (c. 1548).

TRANSLATIONS: Gibson No. XX; Wright No. 39.

REFERENCE: *Rom. hisp.* I, 207-14.

NOTES: Menéndez Pidal says that the transmission of this ballad was a
complicated one. The ballad summarises a long scene of the epic but adds
details not present in that poem. The anticlerical (more strictly, anti-pope)
attitude is probably adopted from the degenerate epic *Mocedades de
Rodrigo* of the 14th century. History knows nothing of any bastard sons
of Fernando I, but the *Crónica de veinte reyes* about 1300 (presumably
drawing on the epic) credits him with 'un fijo de ganançia' who was a
model of ecclesiastical pluralism. There might be here a distant memory
of Drogo, Charlemagne's bastard son who became Archbishop of Metz
(823-55), or, closer to home, of Sancho, son of King Jaime I of Aragon
and brother-in-law of King Alfonso X of Castile-Leon (and not a bastard),
who became Archbishop of Toledo when only doubtfully of age to qualify
(1268-75), owing this post to doubly royal pressure upon the pope. Toledo
was not reconquered from the Muslims until 1085.

15

'Morir os queredes, padre,
¡San Miguel os haya el alma!
Mandastes las vuestras tierras
a quien se vos antojara,
a don Sancho a Castilla,   5
Castilla la bien nombrada,
a don Alonso a León
y a don García a Vizcaya;
a mí, porque soy mujer,
dejáisme desheredada: 10
irme he yo por esas tierras
como una mujer errada,
y este mi cuerpo daría
a quien se me antojara,
a los moros por dineros   15
y a los cristianos de gracia:
¡de lo que ganar pudiere
haré bien por la vuestra alma!'

'¡Calledes, hija, calledes,
no digades tal palabra!   20
que mujer que tal decía
merecía ser quemada.
Allá en Castilla la Vieja
un rincón se me olvidaba:
Zamora había por nombre,   25
Zamora la bien cercada;
de una parte la cerca el Duero,
de otra, peña tajada;
de la otra la Morería
una cosa muy preciada.   30
¡Quien os la tomare, hija,
la mi maldición le caiga!'
Todos dicen: '¡Amén, amén!'
sino don Sancho, que calla.

TEXT: *Prim.* No. 36, from *Silva de varios romances* of 1550.

TRANSLATIONS: Gibson No. XXI; Wright No. 40.

REFERENCES: *Rom. hisp.* I, 210-14; R. Menéndez Pidal, 'Morir vos queredes, padre', *Revista de Filología Española* 2 (1915) 1-20.

NOTES: A number of the best features of the ballad derived from an epic text could be exemplified here, among them the special force of its first lines, spoken by the unnamed and unannounced doña Urraca. Since Zamora was deep in Leonese lands, the king's error in placing it in Old Castile is presumably to be attributed to his weakened mind. As a matter of historical fact the third son, García, received Galicia as his portion of the kingdom, but this name was presumably discarded because it did not fit the assonance in *á-a*. The ballad was highly popular in the Golden Age, and several of its lines became proverbial. Menéndez Pidal has oral versions from Seville, and in Portuguese from the Algarve and the Azores.

16

'¡Afuera, afuera, Rodrigo,
el soberbio castellano!
Acordársete debría
de aquel tiempo ya pasado
cuando fuiste caballero   5
en el altar de Santiago
cuando el rey fue tu padrino,
tú, Rodrigo, el ahijado;
mi padre te dio las armas,

mi madre te dio el caballo,   10
yo te calcé las espuelas
porque fueses más honrado;
que pensé casar contigo,
¡no lo quiso mi pecado!
casaste con Jimena Gómez,   15
hija del conde Lozano,
con ella hubiste dineros,
conmigo hubieras estado.
Bien casaste tú, Rodrigo,
muy mejor fueras casado,   20
dejaste hija de rey
por tomar de su vasallo.'
'Si os parece, mi señora,
bien podemos desligarlo.'
'Mi ánima penaría   25
si yo fuese en discreparlo.'
   '¡Afuera, afuera, los míos,
los de a pie y de a caballo!
pues de aquella torre mocha
una vira me han tirado.   30
No traía el asta hierro,
el corazón me ha pasado;
ya ningún remedio siento
sino vivir más penado.'

TEXT: *Prim.* No. 37, from *Silva de varios romances* of 1550.

TRANSLATIONS: Gibson No. XXX; Wright No. 41.

REFERENCES: *Rom. hisp.* I, 234-6; S.G. Armistead, "'The Enamoured Doña Urraca" in Chronicles and Balladry', *Romance Philology* 11 (1957-8) 26-9.

NOTES: The unannounced speaker is again Doña Urraca. She indignantly rejects the Castilian offer of negotiations made by King Sancho, and tries to shame the Cid, the royal emissary, by mentioning that she had once been so much in love with him that she wished to marry him. The love-affair is shown by Armistead to go back to versions of the epics (in this case the *Mocedades de Rodrigo*) current in the early 14th century; the older *Zamora* epic apparently said merely that the Cid and Urraca had been brought up together as children. The theme of the love-affair acquired even greater prominence in the plays of Guillén de Castro and Corneille. Despite its ultimate epic origin, the ballad has rather late features, such as the mention of Cupid's dart (in the last 8 lines, spoken by the Cid); this, according to Menéndez Pidal, is an example of ballad *novelización*, since in the Zamora epic the Cid, as he approaches the city walls with his message of peace, calls to its defenders not to shoot their *saetas* (darts) at him. The evolution from the large, heroic scene of the epic to the narrow, personal, and sentimental scene of the ballad is noteworthy. The ballad was a favourite in the Golden Age, but is known today only in a Portuguese version from the Algarve.

17

'¡Rey don Sancho, rey don Sancho,
no digas que no te aviso,
que de dentro de Zamora
un alevoso ha salido!
Llámase Vellido Dolfos,   5
hijo de Dolfos Vellido;
cuatro traiciones ha hecho
y con ésta serán cinco.
Si gran traidor fue el padre
mayor traidor es el hijo.'   10
Gritos dan en el real:
'¡A don Sancho han mal herido!
¡Muerto le ha Vellido Dolfos,
gran traición ha cometido!'
Desque le tuviera muerto   15
metióse por un postigo;
por las calles de Zamora
va dando voces y gritos:
'¡Tiempo era, doña Urraca,
de cumplir lo prometido!'   20

TEXT: *Prim.* No. 45, from *Canc. de Rom. 'sin año'* (c. 1548).

TRANSLATION: Wright No. 42.

REFERENCE: *Rom. hisp.* I, 200-1.

NOTES: This ballad is another fine fragment of the *Zamora* epic reduced to a form which is the most brief and tense that can be imagined. The speaker at the start is an unnamed knight who acts at the instigation of Arias Gonzalo, chief of the Zamoran barons and adviser to Urraca. Aware of Dolfos' plan for the salvation of the city, his sense of fair fighting causes him to have a warning about Dolfos' treachery shouted to the besieging Castilians. Dolfos, having killed King Sancho, was received again into the city. In the last two lines the Castilian minstrel, hostile to Urraca's memory, implies that she had been in the secret and had promised Dolfos her favours if he carried out his plan to murder her brother. This may have been true; the monks at Oña, where Sancho was buried, certainly believed she had had a hand in the affair, calling her 'femina mente dira' in the inscription on Sancho's tomb. Such things are not lightly cut in stone by religious persons. The ballad is one of the earliest, already quoted as ancient in the late 15th century, and was often mentioned in the Golden Age.

18

Ya cabalga Diego Ordóñez,
del real se había salido,
de dobles piezas armado
y en un caballo morcillo;
va a retar los zamoranos   5
por la muerte de su primo
que mató Vellido Dolfos
hijo de Dolfos Vellido:
'Yo os rieto, los zamoranos,
por traidores fementidos: 10
rieto a todos los muertos
y con ellos a los vivos;
rieto hombres y mujeres,
los por nacer y nacidos;
rieto a todos los grandes,   15
a los grandes y a los chicos,
a las carnes y pescados
a las aguas de los ríos.'
Allí habló Arias Gonzalo,
bien oiréis lo que hubo dicho: 20
'¿Qué culpa tienen los viejos?
¿qué culpa tienen los niños?
qué merecen las mujeres
y los que no son nacidos?
¿por qué rietas a los muertos,   25
los ganados y los ríos?
Bien sabéis vos, Diego Ordóñez,
muy bien lo tenéis sabido,
que aquél que rieta concejo
debe de lidiar con cinco.'   30
Ordóñez le respondió:
'Traidores heis todos sido.'

TEXT: *Prim.* No. 47, from *Canc. de Rom.* of 1550.

TRANSLATIONS: Gibson No. XXXVI; Wright No. 44.

REFERENCE: *Tratado* I, 352-3.

NOTES: This famous ballad derives from the Zamora epic. The comprehensive challenge-cum-curse reflects very ancient habits of mind and of law, its purpose being to make the whole city feel dishonoured and unclean in every part of its daily life and every member of its population. The belief that for the curse to be effective every detail had to be mentioned is reflected in R.H. Barham's mock-medieval *Jackdaw of Rheims*. See also *Tristram Shandy* III.11.

19

Por aquel postigo viejo
que nunca fuera cerrado,
vi venir pendón bermejo
con trescientos de caballo:
en medio de los trescientos   5
viene un monumento armado,
y dentro del monumento
viene un cuerpo de un finado;
Fernán d'Arias ha por nombre,
hijo de Arias Gonzalo.   10
Llorábanle cien doncellas,
todas ciento hijasdalgo;
todas eran sus parientas
en tercero y cuarto grado;
las unas le dicen primo,   15
otras le llaman hermano;
las otras decían tío,
otras lo llaman cuñado.
Sobre todas lo lloraba
aquesa Urraca Hernando;   20
¡y cuán bien que la consuela
ese viejo Arias Gonzalo!:
'¡Calledes, hija, calledes,
no hagades tan gran llanto!
Que si un hijo me han muerto   25
ahí me quedaban cuatro;
no murió por las tabernas
ni a las tablas jugando,
mas murió sobre Zamora
vuestra honra resguardando.'   30

TEXT: *Prim.* No. 50, from *Canc. de Rom. 'sin año'* (c. 1548).

I: Historical Ballads

TRANSLATIONS: Gibson No. XL; Wright No. 46.

REFERENCE: *Tratado* I, 352-3.

NOTES: This ballad derives from the epic, but is hardly a fragment of it. The five champions of Zamora in the judicial duels were Arias Gonzalo's sons; the series had an inconclusive result, the honour of both sides being partly satisfied, but among those killed was Arias Gonzalo's third son – who seems to have fought first – Fernando (or Hernán). The duels took place, according to local legend reported by Le Strange, in a spot called 'Campo de la Verdad' (that is, God's truth, believed to be revealed in the result of the duels). The small gate in the city walls known as the *Postigo de la Traición* equally survives, and the observer ('vi venir', line 3) is presumably stationed just inside the city and looking out through this opening. The *pendón bermejo* was the banner of Zamora. Oral versions of the ballad have been collected in our century from the Jews of Greece and Asia Minor.

20

En Santa Gadea de Burgos
do juran los hijosdalgo,
allí le toma la jura
el Cid al rey castellano:
las juras eran tan fuertes   5
que al buen rey ponen espanto,
sobre un cerrojo de hierro
y una ballesta de palo:
'Villanos te maten, Alfonso,
villanos, que no hidalgos,   10
de las Asturias de Oviedo,
que no sean castellanos;
mátente con aguijadas,
no con lanzas ni con dardos;
con cuchillos cachicuernos,   15
no con puñales dorados;
abarcas traigan calzadas,
que no zapatos con lazo;
capas traigan aguaderas,
no de contray ni frisado;   20
con camisones de estopa,
no de holanda ni labrados;
caballeros vengan en burras,
que no en mulas ni en caballos;
frenos traigan de cordel,   25

37

que no cueros fogueados;
mátente por las aradas,
que no en villas ni en poblado;
sáquente el corazón
por el siniestro costado,   30
si no dijeres la verdad
de lo que te fuere preguntado,
si fuiste, o consentiste,
en la muerte de tu hermano.'

   Jurado había el rey   35
que en tal nunca se ha hallado;
pero allí hablara el rey
malamente y enojado:
'Muy mal me conjuras, Cid,
Cid, muy mal me has conjurado;   40
mas hoy me tomas la jura,
cras me besarás la mano.'
'Por besar mano de rey
no me tengo por honrado;
porque la besó mi padre   45
me tengo por afrentado.'
'¡Vete de mis tierras, Cid,
mal caballero probado,
y no vengas más a ellas
dende este día en un año!'   50
'Pláceme', dijo el buen Cid,
'Pláceme', dijo, 'de grado,
por ser la primera cosa
que mandas en tu reinado.
Tú me destierras por uno,   55
yo me destierro por cuatro.'

   Ya se parte el buen Cid
sin al rey besar la mano,
con trescientos caballeros
todos eran hijosdalgo;   60
todos son hombres mancebos,
ninguno no había cano.
Todos llevan lanza en puño
y el hierro acicalado,
y llevan sendas adargas   65
con borlas de colorado;
mas no le faltó al buen Cid
adonde asentar su campo.

TEXT: *Prim.* No. 52, from *Canc. de Rom. 'sin año'* (c. 1548).

TRANSLATIONS: Gibson No. XLIII; Wright No. 48 (2).

REFERENCES: *Tratado* I, 354-5; R. Menéndez Pidal, 'En Santa Gadea de Burgos', *Revista de Filología Española* 1 (1914) 357-77; *Rom. hisp.* I, 225-6, and II, 76-7; J. Horrent, 'La jura de Santa Gadea. Historia y poesía', in *Studia Philologica: Homenaje ofrecido a Dámaso Alonso* (Madrid: Gredos, 1960), II, 241-66, reprinted in Horrent's *Historia y poesía en torno al 'Cantar de mio Cid'* (Barcelona: Ariel, 1973), 159-93.

NOTES: The famous 'Jura' cannot be historical fact. There is no reference to it before the 13th century, and it is likely that it was added to the Zamora epic early in that century by a Burgos poet to link the two epics about the Cid and provide an explanation of the hostility between the King and the Cid, which speedily led to the hero's banishment. In both purposes the poet seems to have succeeded admirably. The ballad has suffered some contamination from a line of the *Poema de mio Cid*, and the anti-Asturian note is a rather unfortunate one, perhaps to be explained by the fact that from 1157 to 1230 the kingdoms of Castile and Leon (successor to the kingdom of Asturias) were separate and at times hostile.

The church of Santa Gadea, or Agueda (Agatha) still stands in Burgos, and was one of three specially dedicated *iglesias juraderas*, the others being in Leon city and Avila. It is very small and could not possibly have contained the assembled notables of Castile. It claimed to have among its treasures the ancient *cerrojo* which, with the *ballesta*, presumably provided a mixture of pagan and Christian cross-symbolism. The ballad is known in three 16th-century versions, one from a MS of about 1500. It illustrates the suitability of the verse-form for rapid, vigorous statements and for extensive antithesis.

THE CID

Rodrigo, or Ruy, Díaz de Bivar, known by the honorific title *Cid* or *El Cid* (Arabic *sayyid* 'lord') is the national hero of Spain. Unlike some national heroes, he was a person of solid historical reality who lived from about 1040 until 1099. Legend and poetry gave him a large part to play at the side of Sancho II and in the events at Zamora. In history he was twice banished by Alfonso VI and in exile achieved remarkable successes, most particularly the conquest of the great Muslim-held city of Valencia in 1094. In various 12th-century writings, in the *Poema de mio Cid* (composed probably in or shortly before 1207) and in many later chronicles, he symbolised resistance to an unjust monarch, cheerfulness in exile and adversity, skill in arms, brilliance of generalship and – rather surprisingly – the noble tenderness of father and husband.

Ballads about the Cid are very numerous and have often been gathered into collections. Most are of late date, and none (other than those deriving from the *Zamora* poem) is a good specimen of an epic fragment. The *Poema de mio Cid* had long ceased to be copied, recited or sung when the ballads were being created in the 15th century; none the less, ballads Nos. 21-4 are rather pale reflections of scenes from the *Poema*. The other two Cid ballads derive from the late epic *Mocedades de Rodrigo*, created in the 14th century to entertain listeners who demanded a more romantic hero than the Cid of the old *Poema*. It was in this late epic that the extravagant tales of the Cid's youth were invented, above all the affair with Jimena, which was to enjoy centuries of popularity.

To the Cid, within a vast bibliography, an excellent introduction is that of Richard Fletcher, *The Quest for El Cid* (London: Hutchinson, 1989). The *Poema* is edited by, among others recently, Colin Smith, 3rd ed. (Madrid: Cátedra, 1995). English translations include those of Rita Hamilton & Janet Perry (Harmondsworth: Penguin, 1984), and of Peter Such & John Hodgkinson (Warminster: Aris & Phillips, 1987). On the ballads, see Wright, *CG*, 36-40.

21

¡Hélo, hélo, por do viene!
el moro por la calzada,
caballero a la jineta
encima de una yegua baya,
borceguíes marroquíes   5
y espuela de oro calzada,
una adarga ante los pechos
y en su mano una azagaya.
Mirando estaba a Valencia,
cómo está tan bien cercada: 10
'¡Oh Valencia, oh Valencia,
de mal fuego seas quemada!
Primero fuiste de moros
que de cristianos ganada.
Si la lanza no me miente   15
a moros serás tornada,
aquel perro de aquel Cid
prenderélo por la barba,
su mujer doña Jimena
será de mí cautivada,   20

su hija Urraca Hernando
será mi enamorada,
después de yo harto de ella
la entregaré a mi compaña.'
El buen Cid no está tan lejos   25
que todo bien lo escuchaba:
'Venid vos acá, mi hija,
mi hija doña Urraca;
dejad las ropas continas
y vestid ropas de pascua.   30
Aquel moro hideperro
detenédmelo en palabras,
mientras yo ensillo a Babieca
y me ciño la mi espada.'
La doncella muy hermosa   35
se paró a una ventana:
el moro desque la vido
de esta suerte le hablara:
'¡Alá te guarde, señora,
mi señora, doña Urraca!'   40
'¡Así haga a vos, señor,
buena sea vuestra llegada!
Siete años ha, rey, siete,
que soy vuestra enamorada.'
'Otros tantos ha, señora,   45
que os tengo dentro de mi alma.'
Ellos estando en aquesto
el buen Cid que asomaba:
'¡Adiós, adiós, mi señora,
la mi linda enamorada,   50
que del caballo Babieca
yo bien oigo la patada!'
Do la yegua pone el pie
Babieca pone la pata.
Allí hablara el caballo,   55
bien oiréis lo que hablaba:
'¡Reventar debía la madre
que a su hijo no esperaba!'
Siete vueltas la rodea
al derredor de una jara;   60
la yegua que era ligera
muy adelante pasaba,
hasta llegar cabe un río

adonde una barca estaba.
El moro desque la vido   65
con ella bien se holgaba;
grandes gritos da al barquero
que le allegase la barca;
el barquero es diligente,
túvosela aparejada,   70
embarcó muy presto en ella,
que no se detuvo nada.
Estando el moro embarcado
el buen Cid que llegó al agua,
y por ver al moro en salvo   75
de tristeza reventaba;
mas con la furia que tiene
una lanza le arrojaba
y dijo: '¡Recoged, mi yerno,
arrecogedme esa lanza,   80
que quizá tiempo vendrá
que os será bien demandada!'

TEXT: *Prim.* No. 55, from *Canc. de Rom. 'sin año'* (c. 1548).

TRANSLATIONS: Gibson No. LXXV; Wright No. 50.

REFERENCES: *Tratado* I, 360-6; *Rom. hisp.* I, 226-9, and II, 45-6; P. Bénichou, *Creación poética en el romancero tradicional* (Madrid: Gredos, 1968), 125-59.

NOTES: This episode is a good example of how an epic theme ('King' Búcar's expedition to recover Valencia, lately conquered by the Cid, lines 2311-428 of the *Poema de mio Cid*), is transformed into a romantic, sentimental episode more suited to the taste of later centuries. There might here be some tenuous link with the legend of the daughter of King Didier of Pavia in N. Italy, who offered herself and the city to Charlemagne who was besieging it, according to the *Chronicon Novaliciense* (which was known in some form to a Spanish monk who drew upon it for a Cid-legend) and Paulus Diaconus' *Historia Longobardorum*. It is curious to note that while the epic name of the Cid's horse is accurately preserved, the name of his daughter (in the *Poema* he had two, Elvira and Sol, in history Cristina and María) is here newly invented and is not even a proper patronymic (compare line 20 of ballad No. 19). The famous opening line, with its rapid galloping rhythm, may belong originally to the *Infantes de Lara* cycle (No. 10, line 31), though Armistead thinks it 'simply a recurrent formula'. The ballad exists in several parts of the Peninsula and among the Sephardim in the oral tradition of our century.

22

De concierto están los condes
– hermanos, Diego y Fernando –:
afrentar quieren al Cid,
muy gran traición han armado.
Quieren volverse a sus tierras,   5
sus mujeres han demandado,
y luego su suegro el Cid
se las hubo entregado:
'Mirad, yernos, que tratades
como a dueñas hijasdalgo   10
mis hijas, pues que a vosotros
por mujeres las he dado.'
Ellos ambos le prometen
de obedecer su mandado.
Ya cabalgaban los condes   15
y el buen Cid ya está a caballo
con todos sus caballeros
que le van acompañando;
por las huertas y jardines
van riendo y festejando: 20
por espacio de una legua
el Cid los ha acompañado.
Cuando de ellas se despide
las lágrimas le van saltando;
como hombre que ya sospecha   25
la gran traición que han armado,
manda que vaya tras ellos
Alvar Fáñez su criado.
Vuélvese el Cid y su gente
y los condes van de largo.   30
Andando con muy gran prisa
en un monte habían entrado,
muy espeso, y muy oscuro,
de altos árboles poblado.
Mandaron ir toda su gente   35
adelante muy gran rato.
Quédanse con sus mujeres
tan solos Diego y Fernando.
Apéanse de los caballos
y las riendas han quitado;   40
sus mujeres que lo ven

muy gran llanto han levantado;
apéanlas de las mulas
cada cual para su lado,
como las parió su madre 45
ambas las han desnudado,
y luego a sendas encinas
las han fuertemente atado.
Cada uno azota la suya
con riendas de su caballo: 50
la sangre que de ellas corre
el campo tiene bañado;
mas no contentos con esto
allí se las han dejado.
   Su primo que las hallara 55
como hombre muy enojado
a buscar los condes iba;
como no los ha hallado
volvióse para ellas
muy pensativo y turbado; 60
en casa de un labrador
allí se las ha dejado.
Vase para el Cid su tío,
todo se lo ha contado.
Con muy gran caballería 65
por ellas ha enviado.
De aquesta tan grande afrenta
el Cid al rey se ha quejado;
el rey como aquesto vido
tres Cortes había armado. 70

TEXT: *Prim.* No 57, from *Canc. de Rom. 'sin año'* (c. 1548).

TRANSLATIONS: Gibson No. LXIII; Wright No. 51.

NOTES: This ballad is included as an example of a text which is based on epic material drawn from the chronicles (presumably that printed by Florián de Ocampo in 1541). Its composition filled a gap in the story of the Cid, and the ballad may have been thought of as an essential introduction to the next two poems, Nos. 23 and 24. Although not lacking in good points, there are weak lines and other features which the instinct of minstrels and listeners would have eliminated had the ballad been a traditional one.

23

Por Guadalquivir arriba
cabalgan caminadores,
que – según dicen las gentes –
ellos eran buenos hombres.
Ricas aljubas vestidas,   5
y encima sus albornoces
capas traen aguaderas
a guisa de labradores.
Daban cebada de día
y caminaban de noche,   10
no por miedo de los moros
mas por las grandes calores.
Por sus jornadas contadas
llegados son a las Cortes;
sálelos a recibir   15
el rey con sus altos hombres:
'Viejo que venís, el Cid,
viejo venís y florido.'
'No de holgar con las mujeres,
mas de andar en tu servicio;   20
de pelear con el rey Búcar,
rey que es de gran señorío,
de ganarle sus tierras,
sus villas y sus castillos;
también le gané yo al rey   25
el su escaño tornido.'

TEXT: *Prim.* No 58, from a *pliego suelto* of the 16th century.

REFERENCES: *Rom. hisp.* I, 238; Wright, *CG*, 39.

NOTES: This is a traditional ballad of some antiquity, even though it is not an epic fragment. The Cid's famous *escaño tornido* is mentioned in the *Poema de mio Cid* (lines 3115, 3121, etc.) and much is made of it in later forms of the legend. The Duchess in *Don Quixote* alludes to it as a most honourable seat (II, 33). Mention of the Guadalquivir is an instance of the minstrels' cheerful disregard of geographical fact, since the Cid was (in the *Poema*, at least) on his way from Valencia to the Cortes at Toledo.

24

Tres Cortes armara el rey,
todas tres a una sazón:
las unas armara en Burgos,
las otras armó en León,
las otras armó en Toledo   5
donde los hidalgos son,
para cumplir de justicia
al chico con el mayor.
Treinta días da de plazo,
treinta días, que más no;   10
y el que a la postre viniese
que lo diesen por traidor.
    Veinte y nueve son pasados,
los condes llegados son;
treinta días son pasados   15
y el buen Cid no viene, no.
Allí hablaran los condes:
'Señor, dadlo por traidor.'
Respondiérales el rey:
'Eso no faría, no,   20
que el buen Cid es caballero
de batallas vencedor,
pues que en todas las mis Cortes
no lo había otro mejor.'
    Ellos en aquesto estando   25
el buen Cid que asomó,
con trescientos caballeros
– todos hijosdalgo son –
todos vestidos de un paño,
de un paño y de una color,   30
si no fuera el buen Cid
que traía un albornoz:
'Manténgavos Dios, el rey,
y a vosotros sálveos Dios;
que no hablo yo a los condes,   35
que mis enemigos son.'

TEXT: *Prim.* No. 59, from *Canc. de Rom.* '*sin año*' (c. 1548).

TRANSLATIONS: Gibson No. LXVIII; Wright No. 52.

REFERENCES: *Rom. hisp.* I, 222-4; Wright, *CG*, 39-40.

NOTES: Menéndez Pidal suspected that this ballad derived from a late (14th-century) version of the *Poema de mio Cid*, but there is no evidence for such a reworking, and the poem is best considered a free early invention vaguely based on what the *Poema* says about the Cid's arrival at the Cortes. It is to be noted that the first eight lines of the ballad recall lines 3129-32 of the *Poema* and have the same assonance in *ó(-e)*. The ballad bears the stamp of evolution over a long period in its abruptness and in several stylistic features.

25

En Burgos está el buen rey
asentado a su yantar,
cuando la Jimena Gómez
se le vino a querellar.
Cubierta toda de luto,   5
tocas de negro cendal,
las rodillas por el suelo
comenzara de fablar:
'Con mancilla vivo, rey,
con ella murió mi madre: 10
cada día que amanece
veo al que mató a mi padre
caballero en un caballo
y en su mano un gavilán;
por hacerme más despecho   15
cébalo en mi palomar,
mátame mis palomillas
criadas y por criar,
la sangre que sale de ellas
teñido me ha mi brial.   20
Enviéselo a decir,
envióme a amenazar.
Hacedme, buen rey, justicia,
no me la queráis negar:
rey que no face justicia   25
no debiera de reinar,
ni cabalgar en caballo,
ni con la reina holgar,
ni comer pan a manteles,
ni menos armas armar.'   30
El rey cuando aquesto oyera
comenzara de pensar:
'Si yo prendo o mato al Cid

mis Cortes revolverse han;
pues si lo dejo de hacer   35
Dios me lo ha de demandar;
mandarle quiero una carta
mandarle quiero llamar.'
　Las palabras no son dichas
la carta camino va;   40
mensajero que la lleva
dado la había a su padre.
Cuando el Cid aquesto supo
así comenzó a fablar:
'Malas mañas habéis, conde,   45
no vos las puedo quitar,
que carta que el rey os manda
no me la queréis mostrar.'
'Non era nada, mi fijo,
sino que vades allá;   50
fincad vos acá, mi fijo,
que yo iré en vuestro lugar.'
'Nunca Dios lo tal quisiese,
ni Santa María su madre,
sino que donde vos fuéredes   55
tengo yo de ir delante.'

TEXT: *Prim.* No. 30a, from Timoneda's *Rosa española* of 1573.

TRANSLATIONS: Gibson No. VII; Wright No. 37.

REFERENCES: *Tratado* I, 348-9; *Rom. hisp.* I, 219-20, and II, 74-5; P. Bénichou, 'El casamiento del Cid', *Nueva Revista de Filología Hispánica* 7 (1953) 316-36; A. Montaner Frutos, 'Las quejas de doña Jimena: formación y desarrollo de un tema en la épica y el romancero', in *Actas del II Congreso de la Asociación Hispánica de Literatura Medieval* [1987] (Alcalá de Henares: Universidad Complutense, 1992), 475-507.

NOTES: Two other 16th-century versions of this ballad are known, and it survived in the oral tradition of Andalusia and the Jews of Morocco. It derives, as does the next ballad, from some version of the late epic *Mocedades de Rodrigo* rather different from that which survives and from that which was written into the chronicles.

26

Cabalga Diego Laínez
al buen rey besar la mano,
consigo se los llevaba
los trescientos hijosdalgo.
Entre ellos iba Rodrigo   5
el soberbio castellano.
Todos cabalgan a mula,
sólo Rodrigo a caballo;
todos visten oro y seda,
Rodrigo va bien armado;   10
todos espadas ceñidas,
Rodrigo estoque dorado;
todos con sendas varicas,
Rodrigo lanza en la mano;
todos guantes olorosos,   15
Rodrigo guante mallado;
todos sombreros muy ricos,
Rodrigo casco afinado,
y encima del casco lleva
un bonete colorado.   20
Andando por su camino
unos con otros hablando,
allegados son a Burgos,
con el rey se han encontrado.
Los que vienen con el rey   25
entre sí van razonando,
unos lo dicen de quedo,
otros lo van pregonando:
'Aquí viene entre esta gente
quien mató al conde Lozano.'   30
Como lo oyera Rodrigo
en hito los ha mirado;
con alta y soberbia voz
de esta manera ha hablado:
'Si hay alguno entre vosotros,   35
su pariente o adeudado,
que le pese de su muerte,
salga luego a demandarlo:
yo se lo defenderé
quiera a pie, quiera a caballo.'   40
Todos responden a una:

'Demándelo su pecado.'
   Todos se apearon juntos
para al rey besar la mano;
Rodrigo se quedó sólo   45
encima de su caballo.
Entonces habló su padre,
bien oiréis lo que ha hablado:
'Apeáos vos, mi hijo,
besaréis al rey la mano,   50
porque él es vuestro señor,
vos, hijo, sois su vasallo.'
Desque Rodrigo esto oyó
sintióse más agraviado;
las palabras que responde   55
son de hombre muy enojado:
'Si otro me lo dijera
ya me lo hubiera pagado;
mas por mandarlo vos, padre,
yo lo haré de buen grado.'   60
Ya se apeaba Rodrigo
para al rey besar la mano;
al hincar de la rodilla
el estoque se ha arrancado.
Espantóse de esto el rey,   65
y dijo como turbado:
'¡Quítate, Rodrigo, allá,
quítateme allá, diablo!
que tienes el gesto de hombre
y los hechos de león bravo.'   70
Como Rodrigo esto oyó
aprisa pide el caballo;
con una voz alterada
contra el rey así ha hablado:
'Por besar mano de rey   75
no me tengo por honrado;
porque la besó mi padre
me tengo por afrentado.'
En diciendo estas palabras
salido se ha del palacio;   80
consigo se los tornaba
los trescientos hijosdalgo;
si bien vinieron vestidos
volvieron mejor armados,

y si vinieron en mulas   85
todos vuelven en caballos.

TEXT: *Prim.* No. 29, from *Silva de varios romances* of 1550.

TRANSLATIONS: Lockhart No. 12, 'The Young Cid'; Gibson No. V; Wright No. 38.

REFERENCES: *Tratado* I, 348; *Rom. hisp.* I, 220; Wright, *CG*, 36-7.

NOTES: In the late epic *Mocedades de Rodrigo*, from which this ballad derives, the character of the Cid is very different from that – far nobler, more human, more complex – which we are given in the *Poema de mio Cid*. His contempt for royalty and rather childish display of bad manners in this ballad are all too typical of the *Mocedades* as a whole. As noted earlier, the idea for the lively antithetical section at the start of the ballad may have been borrowed from the Fernán González cycle (No. 8).

FRONTERIZO BALLADS

The *fronterizo* ballads are a specialised group of the *noticiero* or 'news-bearing' ballads of the 14th and 15th centuries (not otherwise represented in this collection as they are of less literary merit). The earliest of these concerns an event of 1312, and they were found useful as propaganda for both sides during the civil wars of the reign of Peter the Cruel (1350-69). The ballad about Baeza, No. 27, is both a part of this civil war poetry and the first *fronterizo* text. The efforts of the regent, Fernando de Antequera, to revive the Reconquest as a national enterprise in the early years of the 15th century stimulated the composition of ballads about it, and the habit of making poetry out of the incidents and personages of the wars against Granada (in which, it has been said, 'the Spanish epic spirit lingered last of all') continued to 1492.

Although literary historians have doubted whether these ballads can be fully contemporary with the events they describe, we may accept Menéndez Pidal's view that they are 'expresión espontánea del sentimiento público, nacidos al calor de los acontecimientos que cantan' if we add that many have suffered later accretions and reworking. They were composed at first by minstrels with the armies and in the service of the nobles, bishops, and *adelantados* (frontier governors) of Andalusia, and later also by court poets and musicians. The ballads have a remarkable unity of tone, and the *brío* and vigour of their battle narrations and harangues are outstanding. So too is their pathos, and their ability to see matters from the Moorish point of view without irony, sarcasm, or contempt – so successfully, indeed, that it was at one time held that certain of these ballads were translated from Arabic originals. Clearly by the 16th century, perhaps earlier, Spaniards were able to appreciate the colourful, exotic aspects of Muslim life and persons by then reckoned less dangerous as enemies.

On these ballads in general, see *Tratado* II, 167-269; *Rom. hisp.* I, 301-16, and II, 6-12; D. Bodmer, *Die granadinischen Romanzen in der europäischen Literatur* (Zürich: Juris, 1955) (on the fame of the ballads in Pérez de Hita's *Guerras civiles de Granada*); Manuel Alvar, *Granada y el romancero* (Granada: Universidad de Granada, 1956); A. García Valdecasas, *El género morisco en las fuentes del 'Romancero general'* (Valencia: Diputación de Valencia, 1987); Wright, *CG*, 41-4. An outstanding study of these ballads in relation to the realities of warfare, social interchange, and politics of the period is that of A. Mackay, 'The Ballad and the Frontier in Late Medieval Spain', *Bulletin of Hispanic Studies* 53 (1976) 15-33.

27

Cercada tiene a Baeza
ese arráez Abdalla Mir,
con ochenta mil peones,
caballeros cinco mil.
Con él va ese traidor   5
el traidor de Pedro Gil.
Por la puerta de Bedmar
la empieza de combatir;
ponen escalas al muro,
comiénzanle a conquerir;   10
ganada tiene una torre,
no le pueden resistir,
cuando de la de Calonge
escuderos vi salir:
Ruy Fernández va delante,   15
aquese caudillo ardid,
arremete con Abdalla
comienza de le ferir,
cortado le ha la cabeza,
los demás dan a fuir.   20

TEXT: *Prim.* No. 18 of Menéndez y Pelayo's *Apéndice I*, from Gonzalo Argote de Molina's *Nobleza de Andalucía* (1588).

TRANSLATION: Wright No. 58.

REFERENCES: *Tratado* II, 169-74; *Rom. hisp.* I, 309, and II, 5.

NOTES: Baeza was besieged in 1368 by the King of Granada, Muhammad V (called Abdalla Mir, or Emir, in the ballad), in alliance with forces of King Peter of Castile (here called Pedro Gil, a contemptuous nickname with connotations of bastardy given him by his enemies). The town was defended by Ruy Fernández de Fuenmayor on behalf of the Pretender, soon to be King Henry II of Trastámara.

28

'Moricos, los mis moricos,
los que ganáis mi soldada,
derribédesme a Baeza
esa villa torreada,
y a los viejos y a los niños   5
los traed en cabalgada,
y a los mozos y varones
los meted todos a espada,
y a ese viejo Pero Díaz
prendédmelo por la barba,   10
y aquesa linda Leonor
será la mi enamorada.
Id vos, capitán Vanegas,
porque venga más honrada,
que si vos sois mandadero   15
será cierta la jornada.'

TEXT: *Prim.* No. 71, from Gonzalo Argote de Molina's *Nobleza de Andalucía* (1588).

REFERENCES: *Tratado* I, 174-6; *Rom. hisp.* II, 9; Wright, *CG*, 44.

NOTES: The Granadan king who, unannounced, orders the attack on Baeza is Muhammad VII, during his campaign against the Christian frontier towns in August 1407. Baeza was defended – successfully – by Pedro Díaz de Quesada. The ballad is ancient but cannot be strictly contemporary, at least in the form in which we have it, since Capitán Vanegas – captured at the age of eight in the Christian town of Luque, and brought up as a Muslim – was not fighting beside the Moors until several decades later. The threats of the monarch against Pedro Díaz and his daughter are clearly taken from a Cid ballad, No. 21.

29

'Reduán, bien se te acuerda
que me diste la palabra
que me darías a Jaén
en una noche ganada.

Reduán, si tú lo cumples   5
daréte paga doblada,
y si tú no lo cumplieres
desterrarte he de Granada;
echarte he en una frontera
do no goces de tu dama.'   10
Reduán le respondía
sin demudarse la cara:
'Si lo dije no me acuerdo,
mas cumpliré mi palabra.'
   Reduán pide mil hombres,   15
el rey cinco mil le daba.
Por esa puerta de Elvira
sale muy gran cabalgada:
¡Cuánto del hidalgo moro!
¡Cuánta de la yegua baya!   20
¡Cuánta de la lanza en puño!
¡Cuánta de la adarga blanca!
¡Cuánta de marlota verde!
¡Cuánta aljuba de escarlata!
¡Cuánta pluma y gentileza!   25
¡Cuánto capellar de grana!
¡Cuánto bayo borceguí!
¡Cuánto lazo que le esmalta!
¡Cuánta de la espuela de oro!
¡Cuánta estribera de plata!   30
Toda es gente valerosa
y experta para batalla.
En medio de todos ellos
va el Rey Chico de Granada.
Míranlo las damas moras   35
de las torres del Alhambra.
La reina mora, su madre,
de esta manera le habla:
'Alá te guarde, mi hijo,
Mahoma vaya en tu guarda,   40
y te vuelva de Jaén
libre, sano y con ventaja,
y te dé paz con tu tío
señor de Guadix y Baza.'

TEXT: *Prim.* No. 72, from Ginés Pérez de Hita's *Guerras civiles de Granada* (2a parte, 1601).

TRANSLATIONS: Lockhart No. 29, 'The Vow of the Moor Reduan'; Wright No. 59.

REFERENCES: *Tratado* II, 176-7; *Rom. hisp.* II, 9-10, 34-5.

NOTES: The attack on Jaén was made in October 1407, on the orders of King Muhammad VII of Granada. Reduán was one of his leading commanders, and he was to perish in the fighting. Only the first part of the ballad can be of early 15th-century date; the second part, with its anachronistic mention of the *Rey Chico* (Boabdil, last king of Granada) may have originated in a description of the departure of Moorish forces on an expedition against Lucena in 1483, the two sections being joined by Pérez de Hita. The lines in which the king's mother addresses and prays for him may have been based on the *Crónica de los Reyes Católicos* by Alonso de Santa Cruz (MS, finished in 1550), in which on the eve of the fall of Granada Boabdil's mother speaks at length with him. The passage is reproduced and translated by C. Smith, *Christians and Moors in Spain* (Warminster: Aris & Phillips, 1989), II, 144-51. Our ballad text is thus, not untypically, a complicated tapestry of interwoven threads and panels (and a 'text' is, etymologically, that which is woven).

30

De Antequera partió el moro
tres horas antes del día,
con cartas en la su mano
en que socorro pedía;
escritas iban con sangre 5
mas no por falta de tinta.
El moro que las llevaba
ciento y veinte años había;
la barba tenía blanca,
la calva le relucía; 10
toca llevaba tocada,
muy grande precio valía;
la mora que la labrara
por su amiga la tenía;
alhaleme en su cabeza 15
con borlas de seda fina;
caballero en una yegua
que caballo no quería.
Solo con un pajecico
que le tenga compañía, 20
no por falta de escuderos

que en su casa hartos había.
Siete celadas le ponen
de mucha caballería,
mas la yegua era ligera,   25
de entre todas se salía;
por los campos de Archidona
a grandes voces decía:
'¡Oh buen rey, si tú supieses
mi triste mensajería   30
mesarías tus cabellos
y la tu barba vellida!'
El rey, que venir lo vido,
a recibirlo salía
con trescientos de caballo   35
la flor de la morería:
'Bien seas venido, el moro,
buena sea tu venida.'
'Alá te mantenga, el rey,
con toda tu compañía.'   40
'Dime, ¿qué nuevas me traes
de Antequera, esa mi villa?'
'Yo te las diré, buen rey,
si tú otorgas la vida.'
'La vida te es otorgada   45
si traición en ti no había.'
'¡Nunca Alá lo permitiese
hacer tan gran villanía!
Mas sepa tu real Alteza
lo que ya saber debría,   50
que esa villa de Antequera
en grande aprieto se vía,
que el infante don Fernando
cercada te la tenía;
fuertemente la combate   55
sin cesar noche ni día.
Manjar que tus moros comen
cueros de vaca cocida;
buen rey, si no la socorres
muy presto se perdería.'   60
    El rey, cuando esto oyera,
de pesar se amortecía;
haciendo gran sentimiento
muchas lágrimas vertía;

rasgaba sus vestiduras 65
con gran dolor que tenía,
ninguno le consolaba
porque no lo permitía;
mas después, en sí tornando,
a grandes voces decía: 70
'Tóquense mis añafiles,
trompetas de plata fina;
júntense mis caballeros
cuantos en mi reino había;
vayan con mis dos hermanos 75
a Archidona, esa mi villa,
en socorro de Antequera,
llave de mi señoría.'
　　Y así con este mandado
se juntó gran morería: 80
ochenta mil peones fueron
el socorro que venía,
con cinco mil de caballo,
los mejores que tenía.
Así en la Boca del Asna 85
este real sentado había
a vista dél del infante
el cual ya se apercibía,
confiando en la gran victoria
que de ellos Dios le daría, 90
sus gentes bien ordenadas.
De San Juan era aquel día
cuando se dio la batalla
de los nuestros tan herida,
que por ciento y veinte muertos 95
quince mil moros había.
Después de aquesta batalla
fue la villa combatida
con lombardas y pertrechos
y con una gran bastida, 100
con que le ganan las torres
de donde era defendida.
Después dieron el castillo
los moros a pleitesía,
que libres con sus haciendas 105
el infante les pondría
en la villa de Archidona,

lo cual todo se cumplía:
y así se ganó Antequera
a loor de Santa María.   110

TEXT: *Prim.* No. 74, from *Canc. de Rom. 'sin año'* (c. 1548).

TRANSLATION: Wright No. 60.

REFERENCES: *Tratado* II, 179-82; *Rom. hisp.* I, 307, and II, 7; F. López
Estrada, 'La conquista de Antequera en el romancero y en la épica de
los Siglos de Oro', *Anales de la Universidad Hispalense* 16 (1955)
133-92; Wright, *CG*, 45-7; on this ballad in the modern oral tradition,
see S.G. Armistead in *Nueva Revista de Filología Hispánica* 13 (1959)
88-97.

NOTES: The conquest of Antequera, an ancient town of great strategic
importance, by the Regent don Fernando ('de Antequera') in 1410 was the
outstanding event of its time. The siege lasted five months; the relieving
army was defeated with immense slaughter on 16 May, and on 28 September
the city surrendered. According to Menéndez Pidal, the first 74 lines
are of early 15th-century date, but the final portion, with its relative clauses
and unhappy syntax, is a late addition made from the *Crónica de don Juan
II*. Indeed, the style of the military communiqué from line 85 onward is
somewhat remote from that of the traditional ballad.

31

La mañana de San Juan
al tiempo que alboreaba,
gran fiesta hacen los moros
por la Vega de Granada.
Revolviendo sus caballos   5
y jugando de las lanzas,
ricos pendones en ellas
broslados por sus amadas,
ricas marlotas vestidas
tejidas de oro y grana.   10
El moro que amores tiene
señales de ello mostraba,
y el que no tenía amores
allí no escaramuzaba.
Las damas moras los miran   15
de las torres del Alhambra;
también se los mira el rey
de dentro de la Alcazaba.
Dando voces vino un moro

con la cara ensangrentada: 20
'Con tu licencia, el rey,
te diré una nueva mala:
el infante don Fernando
tiene a Antequera ganada;
muchos moros deja muertos, 25
yo soy quien mejor librara;
siete lanzadas yo traigo,
el cuerpo todo me pasan;
los que conmigo escaparon
en Archidona quedaban.' 30
   Con la tal nueva el rey
la cara se le demudaba;
manda juntar sus trompetas
que toquen todas al arma;
manda juntar a los suyos, 35
hace muy gran cabalgada,
y a las puertas de Alcalá
que la Real se llamaba,
los cristianos y los moros
una escaramuza traban. 40
Los cristianos eran muchos,
mas llevaban orden mala;
los moros, que son de guerra,
dádoles han mala carga;
de ellos matan, de ellos prenden, 45
de ellos toman en celada.
Con la victoria los moros
van la vuelta de Granada;
a grandes voces decían:
'¡La victoria ya es cobrada!' 50

TEXT: *Prim.* No. 75, from *Silva de varios romances* of 1550.

REFERENCES: *Tratado* II, 182; *Rom. hisp.* II, 10 and 35-6; Wright, *CG*, 47.

NOTES: Menéndez Pidal points out that the first part of this ballad is much later than the second, since it derives from a poem about Jarifa and Abindarráez (in turn based on a famous prose tale of the mid-16th century) and is more in accord with the sentimental *morisco* ballads of the late 16th century. Although it is certain that the Muslims celebrated the festivity of Midsummer (christianised as St John's Day) despite the prohibition of their religious leaders, Antequera in fact fell in late September, the ballads very properly taking no account of such things in their instinct for evocative opening lines. Alcalá la Real ('Real', because captured by Alfonso XI in person in 1340) was a Christian outpost some 40 km north-west of Granada.

32

Caballeros de Moclín,
peones de Colomera,
entrado habían en acuerdo
en su consejada negra
a los campos de Alcalá   5
donde irían a hacer presa.
Allá la van a hacer
a esos molinos de Huelma.
Derrocaban los molinos,
derramaban la cibera,   10
prendían los molineros
cuantos hay en la ribera.
  Ahí hablara un viejo
que era más discreto en guerra:
'Para tanto caballero   15
chica cabalgada es ésta;
soltemos un prisionero
que a Alcalá lleve la nueva;
démosle tales heridas
que en llegando luego muera;   20
cortémosle el brazo derecho
porque no nos haga guerra.'
Por soltar un molinero
un mancebo les saliera
que era nacido y criado   25
en Jerez de la Frontera,
que corre más que un gamo
y salta más que una cierva.
Por los campos de Alcalá
diciendo va: '¡Afuera, afuera!   30
caballeros de Alcalá
no os alabaréis de aquésta,
que por una que hicistes
y tan cara como cuesta,
que los moros de Moclín   35
corrido vos han la ribera,
robado vos han el campo

60

y llevado vos han la presa.'
Oídolo ha don Pedro
por su desventura negra: 40
cabalgara en su caballo
que le decían Bocanegra;
al salir de la ciudad
encontró con Sayavedra:
'No vayades allá, hijo,   45
si mi maldición os venga;
que si hoy fuere la suya
mañana será la vuestra.'

TEXT: *Prim.* No. 77, from *Canc. de Rom.* of 1550.

REFERENCE: Wright, *CG*, 47.

NOTES: The ballad as often stops short of the factual dénouement which
the modern reader expects: that don Pedro Fernández de Córdoba, he of
the 'desventura negra', did not heed the warning of his father don Diego
Fernández, spoken in the last four lines, but led his men out of Alcalá
and fell into the enemy trap, and was killed. The incident took place in
June 1424.

33

'¡Abenámar, Abenámar,
moro de la morería,
el día que tú naciste
grandes señales había!
Estaba la mar en calma,   5
la luna estaba crecida;
moro que en tal signo nace
no debe decir mentira.'
Allí respondiera el moro,
bien oiréis lo que decía: 10
'Yo te la diré, señor,
aunque me cueste la vida,
porque soy hijo de un moro
y una cristiana cautiva;
siendo yo niño y muchacho   15
mi madre me lo decía,
que mentira no dijese,
que era grande villanía:
por tanto pregunta, rey,
que la verdad te diría.'   20

'Yo te agradezco, Abenámar,
aquesa tu cortesía.
¿Qué castillos son aquéllos?
¡Altos son y relucían!'
'El Alhambra era, señor,   25
y la otra la mezquita;
los otros los Alixares
labrados a maravilla;
el moro que los labraba
cien doblas ganaba al día,   30
y el día que nos los labra
otras tantas se perdía.
El otro el Generalife,
huerta que par no tenía;
el otro Torres Bermejas,   35
castillo de gran valía.'
    Allí habló el rey don Juan,
bien oiréis lo que decía:
'Si tú quisieses, Granada,
contigo me casaría: 40
daréte en arras y dote
a Córdoba y a Sevilla.'
    'Casada soy, rey don Juan,
casada soy, que no viuda;
el moro que a mí me tiene   45
muy grande bien me quería.'

TEXT: *Prim.* No. 78a, from Ginés Pérez de Hita's *Guerras civiles de Granada* (2a parte, 1601).

TRANSLATIONS: by Southey, published in *Modern Language Notes* 34 (1919) 333-4; Gibson p. 337; Wright (from a greatly varying but equally good version) No. 62; and in French by Chateaubriand, 'Le Roi don Jean' in *Le Dernier Abencérage*.

REFERENCES: *Tratado* II, 186-92; L. Spitzer, 'El romance de *Abenámar*', *Asomante* [Puerto Rico] 1 (1945) 7-29, reprinted in *Sobre antigua poesía española* (Buenos Aires: Universidad de Buenos Aires, 1962), 61-84; P. Bénichou, *Creación poética en el romancero tradicional* (Madrid: Gredos, 1968), 61-92; J. Torres Fontes, 'La historicidad del romance *Abenámar, Abenámar*', *Anuario de Estudios Medievales* 8 (1972-3) 225-56; J. Victorio, 'La ciudad-mujer en los romances fronterizos', *Anuario de Estudios Medievales* 15 (1986) 553-60; Wright, *CG*, 48-50; A. Alvarez Sanagustín, 'La composición artística: el romance de Abenámar', in *Homenaje a Alvaro Galmés de Fuentes*, 3 vols (Oviedo: Universidad de Oviedo, and Madrid: Gredos, 1985-7), III, 293-302; C. Smith, *Christians and Moors in Spain*, 2 vols (Warminster: Aris & Phillips, 1989), II, 122-33, for this ballad, the Mena passage, and a chronicle account, with translations.

NOTES: In this famous ballad King John II of Castile questions Abenámar (Yusuf Ibn al-Mawl), pretender to the throne of Granada and supported by the Christians, about the great buildings of the city which they can see from a hill outside it. The stupendous view is not greatly changed today. It was on 27 June 1431 that the Christian army came within sight of the city; it later fought and won the battle of La Higueruela, which was to be poetically evoked by Juan de Mena in his *Laberinto de Fortuna* (1444; stanzas 148-51). Abenámar ruled briefly in Granada in 1431-2 as a vassal of King John, but was soon overthrown and executed. Pérez de Hita's version of the text is better than others printed in the 16th century, which continue the story rather prosaically after the reply of 'Granada'. This personification, and the pleasant fiction of the city being the 'bride' of her ruler, are borrowed from Arabic poetry and for long led scholars to assume that the ballad was translated from an Arabic original, but it is now agreed that this was not so.

34

Álora, la bien cercada,
tú que estás en par del río,
cercóte el adelantado
una mañana en domingo,
de peones y hombres de armas 5
el campo bien guarnecido,
con la gran artillería
hecho te había un portillo.
Viérades moros y moras
todos huir al castillo; 10
las moras llevaban ropa,
los moros harina y trigo,
y las moras de quince años
llevaban el oro fino,
y los moricos pequeños 15
llevaban la pasa e higo.
Por cima de la muralla
su pendón llevan tendido.
Entre almena y almena
quedado se había un morico 20
con una ballesta armada

y en ella puesto un cuadrillo.
En altas voces decía
que la gente lo había oído:
'¡Treguas, treguas, adelantado,   25
por tuyo se da el castillo!'
Alza la visera arriba
por ver el que tal le dijo;
asestárale a la frente,
salido le ha al colodrillo.   30
Sacóle Pablo de rienda,
y de mano Jacobillo,
estos dos que había criado
en su casa desde chicos;
lleváronle a los maestros   35
por ver si será guarido;
a las primeras palabras
el testamento les dijo.

TEXT: *Prim.* No. 79, from a *pliego suelto* of the 16th century.

TRANSLATION: Wright No. 63.

REFERENCES: *Tratado* II, 193-4; J. Battesti, 'El romance ¿modelo de
escritura? Análisis del romance de *Álora la bien cercada*', *Prohemio* 6
(1975) 21-44; A.D. Deyermond, '*Álora la bien cercada*: Structure, Image,
and Point of View in a Frontier Ballad', in *Hispanic Medieval Studies in
Honor of Samuel G. Armistead* (Madison: Hispanic Seminary of Medieval
Studies, 1992), 97-109; Wright, *CG*, 50-1.

NOTES: Álora, on the Guadalhorce north-west of Málaga, was besieged
by the *adelantado* don Diego de Ribera in May of 1434. As already noted,
Mena knew this or similar poems when writing his *Laberinto* (1444; see
stanza 190).

35

Día era de San Antón,
ese santo señalado,
cuando salen de Jaén
cuatrocientos hijosdalgo;
y de Úbeda y Baeza   5
se salían otros tantos,
mozos deseosos de honra
y los más enamorados.
En brazos de sus amigas
van todos juramentados   10

de no volver a Jaén
sin dar moro en aguinaldo.
La seña que ellos llevaban
es pendón rabo de gallo;
por capitán se lo llevan   15
al obispo don Gonzalo,
armado de todas armas
en un caballo alazano;
todos se visten de verde,
el obispo azul y blanco.   20
   Al castillo de la Guardia
el obispo había llegado;
sáleselo a recibir
Mexía, el noble hidalgo:
'Por Dios te ruego, el obispo,   25
que no pasades el vado,
porque los moros son muchos,
a la Guardia habían llegado;
muerto me han tres caballeros,
de que mucho me ha pesado;   30
el uno era tío mío
el otro mi primo hermano,
y el otro es un pajecico
de los míos más preciados.'
'Demos la vuelta, señores,   35
demos la vuelta a enterrarlos,
haremos a Dios servicio,
honraremos los cristianos.'
   Ellos estando en aquesto
llegó don Diego de Haro: 40
'Adelante, caballeros,
que me llevan el ganado;
si de algún villano fuera
ya lo hubiérades quitado;
empero alguno está aquí   45
que le place de mi daño;
no cumple decir quién es,
que es el del roquete blanco.'
   El obispo, que lo oyera,
dio de espuelas al caballo;   50
el caballo era ligero,
saltado había un vallado;
mas al salir de una cuesta

a la asomada de un llano,
vido mucha adarga blanca,   55
mucho albornoz colorado,
y muchos hierros de lanzas
que relucían en el campo;
metídose había por ellos
como león denodado;   60
de tres batallas de moros
la una ha desbaratado,
mediante la buena ayuda
que en los suyos ha hallado;
aunque algunos de ellos mueren   65
eterna fama han ganado.
Los moros son infinitos,
al obispo habían cercado;
cansado de pelear
lo derriban del caballo,   70
y los moros victoriosos
a su rey lo han presentado.

TEXT: *Prim*. No. 82, from Gonzalo Argote de Molina's *Nobleza de Anda-
lucía* (1588).

REFERENCES: *Tratado* II, 204-9; Menéndez Pidal, 'Un día de San Antón', *Revista
de Filología Española* 2 (1915) 112-36; *Rom. hisp*. I, 315; Wright, *CG*, 51-2.

NOTES: The Bishop of Jaén who set off on this sporting raid on St
Anthony's Day (17 January) in about 1435 was the famous don Gonzalo
de Zúñiga. A 17th-century historian recorded a snatch of song about him
to the effect that 'suele decir misa armado', and he was of the line of
fighting bishops that included Jerónimo of Valencia (*Poema de mio Cid*)
and Turpin of Rheims (*Chanson de Roland*, etc.). The raid was, as a matter
of history, successful, and the dramatic ending of the ballad with its tale
of the bishop's capture is the result of contamination with another text.
Legend is firm, however, in believing that the cleric was not only captured,
but refused to be ransomed and died a captive in Granada (in fact he died
in peaceful retirement in Seville in 1456 or 1457).

36

'Dadme nuevas, caballeros,
nuevas me querades dar
de aquese conde de Niebla
don Enrique de Guzmán,
que hace guerra a los moros   5

y ha cercado a Gibraltar.
Veo hoy lutos en mi corte,
ayer vi fiestas muy grandes:
o el príncipe es fallecido
o alguno de mi sangre,
o don Alvaro de Luna,
el maestre y condestable.'
    'No es muerto, señora, el príncipe,
mas ha fallecido un grande,
que veredes a los moros
cuán poco vos temerán,
que a este solo temían
y no osaban saltear;
es el buen conde de Niebla
que se ha anegado en la mar,
por acorrer a los suyos
nunca se quiso salvar;
en un batel donde venía
le hicieron trastornar,
socorriendo un caballero
que se le iba a anegar;
la mar andaba tan alta
que no se pudo escapar,
teniendo casi ganada
la fuerza de Gibraltar.
Lloranle todas las damas,
galanes otro que tal,
llorale gente de guerra
por ser tan buen capitán,
lloranle duques y condes
porque a todos sabía honrar.'
    '¡Oh qué nuevas me traedes,
caballeros, de pesar!
Vístanse todos de jerga,
no se hagan fiestas más,
vaya luego un mensajero,
venga su hijo don Juan;
confirmarle he lo del padre,
más le quiero acrecentar,
y de Medina Sidonia
duque le hago de hoy más,
que a hijo de tan buen padre
poco galardón se da.'

10
15
20
25
30
35
40
45

TEXT: *Prim.* No. 80, from *Silva de varios romances* of 1550.

TRANSLATION: Wright No. 64.

REFERENCES: *Tratado* II, 195-6; Wright, *CG*, 52-3.

NOTES: The Conde de Niebla's ill-fated expedition against Gibraltar took place in May 1436; it seems that tragedy resulted from the simple failure to reckon with the height of the tides. The incident is splendidly told by Juan de Mena in his *Laberinto* (stanzas 160-86). According to Menéndez y Pelayo this ballad in its present form is not contemporary with the event since it contains reminiscences of a lament for the death of Prince Alonso in 1491.

37

Jugando estaba el rey moro
y aun al ajedrez un día,
con aquese buen Fajardo
con amor que le tenía.
Fajardo jugaba a Lorca   5
y el rey moro a Almería;
jaque le dio con el roque,
el alférez le prendía.
A grandes voces dice el moro:
'¡La villa de Lorca es mía!'   10
Allí hablara Fajardo,
bien oiréis lo que decía:
'Calles, calles, señor rey,
no tomes la tal porfía;
que aunque me la ganases   15
ella no se te daría;
caballeros tengo dentro
que te la defenderían.'
Allí hablara el rey moro,
bien oiréis lo que decía: 20
'No juguemos más, Fajardo,
ni tengamos más porfía,
que sois tan buen caballero
que todo el mundo os temía.'

TEXT: *Prim.* No. 83, from *Canc. de Rom. 'sin año'* (c. 1548).

TRANSLATION: Wright No. 65 (variant version).

REFERENCES: *Tratado* II, 201-4; E. Buceta, 'Anotaciones sobre la identificación del Fajardo en el romance...', *Revista de Filología Española* 17 (1931) 24-33; J. Torres Fontes, 'El Fajardo del *Romance del juego de ajedrez*', *Revista Bibliográfica y Documental* 2 (1948) 305-14; Wright, *CG*, 53-4.

NOTES: This ballad is obviously pure fiction, but even fiction has its *raison d'être*: in this case the friendship between the *adelantado* Pedro Fajardo and the last kings of Granada. The story of the chess game may derive from an anecdote of the Arab historians about a match played between Alfonso VI and the vizier of King Al-Mutamid of Seville in the late 11th century, according to Menéndez y Pelayo, in which Alfonso lost with a better grace than Fajardo.

38

'Moro alcaide, moro alcaide,
el de la vellida barba,
el rey te manda prender
por la pérdida de Alhama,
y cortarte la cabeza   5
y ponerla en el Alhambra
porque a ti sea castigo
y otros tiemblen en mirarla,
pues perdiste la tenencia
de una ciudad tan preciada.'   10
El alcalde respondía,
de esta manera les habla:
'Caballeros y hombres buenos,
los que regís a Granada,
decid de mi parte al rey   15
como no le debo nada;
yo me estaba en Antequera,
en bodas de una mi hermana:
¡mal fuego queme las bodas
y quien a ellas me llamara!   20
El rey me dio su licencia,
que yo no me la tomara;
pedíla por quince días,
diómela por tres semanas.
De haberse Alhama perdido   25
a mí me pesa en el alma,
que si el rey perdió su tierra
yo perdí mi honra y fama;
perdí hijos y mujer,

las cosas que más amaba; 30
perdí una hija doncella
que era la flor de Granada.
El que la tiene cautiva
marqués de Cádiz se llama:
cien doblas le doy por ella, 35
no me las estima en nada;
la respuesta que me han dado
es que mi hija es cristiana,
y por nombre le habían puesto
doña María de Alhama; 40
el nombre que ella tenía
mora Fátima se llama.'
   Diciendo esto el alcaide
le llevaron a Granada,
y siendo puesto ante el rey 45
la sentencia le fue dada:
que le corten la cabeza
y la lleven al Alhambra.
Ejecutóse justicia
así como el rey lo manda. 50

TEXT: *Prim.* No. 84a, from Ginés Pérez de Hita's *Guerras civiles de Granada* (2a parte, 1601).

TRANSLATION: Wright No. 67.

REFERENCES: *Tratado* II, 211-12; Wright, *CG*, 55-6; on this ballad in the modern oral tradition, see S.G. Armistead in *Nueva Revista de Filología Hispánica* 13 (1959) 88-97.

NOTES: An earlier version of this ballad, only 16 lines long, was printed in 1550; but against the usual rule, there seems good reason in this case to prefer Pérez de Hita's fuller text. He calls it a 'sentido y antiguo romance', and indeed he seems to have printed it without adding exotic or sentimental notes as he often did. The ballad includes the logical dénouement of the story, unlike many of our texts; but in its plainness it conveys all the pathos of war. Alhama was stormed in a night attack on 28 February 1482, by the troops of don Rodrigo Ponce de León, Marquis of Cádiz. The town lies some 45 km south-west of Granada.

39

Paseábase el rey moro
por la ciudad de Granada,
desde la puerta de Elvira

hasta la de Vivarambla.
(¡Ay de mi Alhama!)   5
Cartas le fueron venidas
que Alhama era ganada;
las cartas echó en el fuego
y al mensajero matara.
(¡Ay de mi Alhama!)   10
Descabalga de una mula
y en un caballo cabalga;
por el Zacatín arriba
subido se había al Alhambra.
(¡Ay de mi Alhama!)   15
Como en el Alhambra estuvo
al mismo punto mandaba
que se toquen sus trompetas,
sus añafiles de plata.
(¡Ay de mi Alhama!)   20
Y que las cajas de guerra
aprisa toquen al arma,
porque lo oigan sus moros
los de la Vega y Granada.
(¡Ay de mi Alhama!)   25
    Los moros que el son oyeron
que al sangriento Marte llama,
uno a uno y dos a dos
juntado se ha gran batalla.
(¡Ay de mi Alhama!)   30
Allí habló un moro viejo
de esta manera hablara:
'¿Para qué nos llamas, rey,
para qué es esta llamada?'
(¡Ay de mi Alhama!)   35
    'Habéis de saber, amigos,
una nueva desdichada:
que cristianos de braveza
ya nos han ganado Alhama.'
(¡Ay de mi Alhama!)   40
    Allí habló un alfaquí
de barba crecida y cana:
'¡Bien se te emplea, buen rey,
buen rey, bien se te empleara!
(¡Ay de mi Alhama!)   45
Mataste los Bencerrajes

que eran la flor de Granada,
cogiste los tornadizos
de Córdoba la nombrada.
(¡Ay de mi Alhama!)   50
Por eso mereces, rey,
una pena muy doblada:
que te pierdas tú y el reino
y aquí se pierda Granada.'
(¡Ay de mi Alhama!)   55

TEXT: *Prim.* No. 85a, from Ginés Pérez de Hita's *Guerras civiles de Granada* (2a parte, 1601).

TRANSLATIONS: Gibson p. 340; by Byron, 'The Moorish king rides up and down' (1818), a neat and spirited version marred by one or two disastrous lines. (It includes the previous ballad, No. 38, as a second part.)

REFERENCES: *Tratado* II, 209-11; *Rom. hisp.* II, 33-4, 85, and 132; J.F.G. Gornall, 'El rey moro que perdió Alhama: The Origin of the Famous Version', *Romance Notes* 22 (1982) 324-8; Wright, *CG*, 56-7.

NOTES: With its exceptional tragic refrain (not the invention of Pérez de Hita, but recorded in songbooks of 1538 and 1552, etc.), this ballad is more lyrical than narrative. It was a favourite with Golden Age musicians and poets, and a much-altered oral version was picked up in Seville in 1916. Pérez de Hita's claim that the ballad had an Arabic original was accepted by some scholars, but is denied by Menéndez Pidal; this does not rule out the existence of other Arabic laments for the loss of Alhama. Other versions without the refrain were printed in the 16th century. The aged *alfaquí* who prophesies the fall of Granada as punishment for the king's injustice refers to the massacre, some years before, of the Abencerraje tribe (suspected of treachery), and the acceptance into royal favour of the Cordobese *tornadizos* or renegades of Christian origin, known by the tribal name of the Cegríes. The story of the struggle between these groups forms a large part of the *Guerras civiles de Granada*.

40

Sobre Baza estaba el rey,
lunes, después de yantar;
miraba las ricas tiendas
que estaban en su real;
miraba las huertas grandes   5
y miraba el arrabal,
miraba el adarve fuerte
que tenía la ciudad,

72

miraba las torres espesas
que no las puede contar.   10
Un moro tras una almena
comenzóle de fablar:
'Vete, el rey don Fernando,
no querrás aquí invernar,
qué los fríos desta tierra   15
no los podrás comportar;
pan tenemos por diez años,
mil vacas para salar;
veinte mil moros hay dentro,
todos de armas tomar,   20
ochocientos de caballo
para el escaramuzar;
siete caudillos tenemos
tan buenos como Roldán,
y juramento tienen hecho   25
antes morir que se dar.'

TEXT: *Prim.* No. 23 of *Apéndice* I, from Barbieri, *Cancionero musical de los siglos XV y XVI.*

REFERENCES: *Tratado* II, 213-14; *Rom. hisp.* II, 21-32; Wright, *CG*, 57-8.

NOTES: Menéndez Pidal says that this ballad was composed in its tense, truncated form, probably by one of the court musicians, and that it was sung at the festivities which greeted Queen Isabel when she arrived at the Christian camp outside Baza on 5 November 1489. The anonymous poet succeeds brilliantly in seeing matters from the Moorish point of view. However difficult the siege may have seemed at this time, the attackers were able to force the surrender of the town a few weeks later, on 4 December.

II

CAROLINGIAN BALLADS

It is one of the striking facts of literary history that Spanish poets were able to put to such good and abundant use the Carolingian material which had originated in France but which was, by the 15th century, no longer much esteemed there. In a similar way but on a larger scale, the Arthurian materials of Britain caught the imagination of artists all over Europe, particularly in France. The two worlds – of Arthur and Charlemagne – were indeed not so very dissimilar by the end of the Middle Ages, and the vogue for the Carolingian ballads in Spain in the 15th and 16th centuries was accompanied by the vogue for the tales of Amadís and his progeny in prose. The two worlds at times became one in the impressionable brain of Don Quixote.

This is not the place to discuss the way in which the Carolingian material evolved in France, since this would be to enter the still unresolved debate about the origins and development of French epic. The legends appear as highly-wrought *chansons de geste* in the 12th and 13th centuries, the great *Chanson de Roland* being then as now the best known. Various of these epics were known in Spain, either in their original language among the colonies of French settlers (many of these having come as pilgrims to Compostela) established in many Spanish towns, or in Spanish verse adaptations such as the Navarrese *Roncesvalles* of which a 100-line fragment survives. From these epics, as from the Spanish ones, portions were reworked and developed as ballads of the brief and sometimes truncated kind (Nos. 41-9). The others (Nos. 50-4) are of the species called *juglarescos*; they have no epic origin, but are new creations by the 15th-century minstrels, more romantic and extravagant in theme and more purely narrative in style.

On the Carolingian ballads, see *Tratado* II, 320-45; *Rom. hisp.* I, 244-300; J. Horrent, 'Sur les romances carolingiens de Roncevaux', *Les Lettres Romanes* 9 (1955) 161-76; O.R. Ochrymowycz, *Aspects of Oral Style in the 'Romances juglarescos' of the Carolingian Cycle* (Iowa City: University of Iowa, 1975); Wright, *CG*, 59-60; S.G. Armistead & J.H. Silverman, *Judeo-Spanish Ballads from Oral Tradition. II. Carolingian Ballads (1): Roncesvalles*, Folk Literature of the Sephardic Jews, 3 (Berkeley: University of California Press, 1994).

41

Ya comienzan los franceses
con los moros pelear,
y los moros eran tantos
no los dejan resollar.
Allí habló Baldovinos,   5
bien oiréis lo que dirá:
'Ay compadre don Beltrán
mal nos va en esta batalla,
más de sed que no de hambre,
a Dios quiero yo dar el alma;   10
cansado traigo el caballo,
más, el brazo de la espada;
roguemos a don Roldán
que una vez el cuerno taña,
oírlo ha el emperador   15
que está en los puertos de España,
que más vale un socorro
que toda nuestra sonada.'
Oídolo ha don Roldán
en las batallas do estaba: 20
'No me lo roguéis, mis primos,
que ya rogado me estaba,
mas rogadlo a don Reinaldos
que a mí no me lo retraiga,
ni me lo retraiga en villa   25
ni me lo retraiga en Francia
ni en cortes del emperador
estando comiendo a la tabla,
que más querría ser muerto
que sufrir tal sobarbada.'   30
Oídolo ha don Reinaldos
que en las batallas andaba;
comenzara a decir,
estas palabras hablaba:
'¡Oh mal hubiesen franceses   35
de Francia, la natural,
que a tan pocos moros como éstos
el cuerno mandan tocar,
que si me toman los corajes
que me solían tomar,   40
por éstos y otros tantos

no me daré sólo un pan!'
   Ya le toman los corajes
que le solían tomar;
así se entra por los moros   45
como segador por pan,
así derriba cabezas
como peras de un peral;
por Roncesvalles arriba
los moros huyendo van.   50
Allí salió un perro moro
que mala hora lo parió su madre:
'¡Alcarria, moros, alcarria,
si mala rabia vos mate!
que sois ciento para uno   55
irles huyendo delante;
¡Oh mal haya el rey Marsín
que soldada os manda dar;
mal haya la reina mora
que vos la manda pagar;   60
mal hayáis vosotros, moros,
que la venís a ganar!'
   De que esto oyeron los moros
aun ellos volvido se han,
y vueltas y revueltas   65
los franceses huyendo van.
Atán bien se los esfuerza
ese arzobispo Turpín:
   '¡Vuelta, vuelta, los franceses,
con corazón a la lid;   70
más vale morir con honra
que con deshonra vivir!'
   Ya volvían los franceses
con corazón a la lid;
tantos matan de los moros   75
que no se puede decir;
por Roncesvalles arriba
huyendo va el rey Marsín,
caballero en una cebra
no por mengua de rocín;   80
la sangre que dél salía
las yerbas hace teñir,
las voces que él iba dando
al cielo quieren subir:

'Reniego de ti, Mahoma   85
y aun de cuanto hice en ti;
hícete el cuerpo de plata,
pies y manos de marfil,
y por más te honrar, Mahoma,
la cabeza de oro te hiz.   90
Sesenta mil caballeros
ofrecílos yo a ti,
mi mujer Abrayma mora
ofrecióte treinta mil,
mi hija Mataleona   95
ofrecióte quince mil;
de todos éstos, Mahoma,
tan solo me veo aquí,
y aun mi brazo derecho
Mahoma, no lo traigo aquí,   100
cortómelo el encantado
ese Roldán paladín,
que si encantado no fuera
no se me fuera él así;
mas yo me iré para Roma   105
que cristiano quiero morir,
ése será mi padrino
ese Roldán paladín,
ése me bautizará
ese arzobispo Turpín;   110
mas perdóname, Mahoma,
que con cuita te lo dije;
que ir no quiero a Roma,
curar quiero yo de mí.'

TEXT: *Prim.* No. 50 of Menéndez y Pelayo's *Apéndice* I, from a *pliego suelto* of the 16th century.

TRANSLATION: Wright No. 31.

REFERENCES: On this and the next ballad see *Tratado* II, 364-8; *Rom. hisp.* I, 246-8; J. Horrent, *La Chanson de Roland dans les littératures française et espagnole au moyen âge* (Paris: Les Belles Lettres, 1951), 504-8; Wright, *CG*, 60-2.

NOTES: Scholars are agreed that this ballad represents a section of the *Roncesvalles* epic, which was an adaptation of some late (and now lost) version of the *Chanson de Roland*; but Don Beltrán already figures as *Bertlane*, a companion of Roland, in the 11th-century *Nota Emilianense*

which summarises a very early Peninsular (Navarrese?) version of the
Roland story. The ballad abbreviates the epic text considerably, but re-
mains faithful to it in several details. Marsín is the *Marsilie* of the French
poem, Muslim king of Saragossa. Don Reinaldos (de Montalván) is not
present in the French tradition, but already figured in the Spanish *Ronces-
valles* as we know from the fragment of it which survives. The false idea
that the Muslims worshipped images of Muhammad is present in the
French traditions, so powerfully that the Spaniards – who knew their
Muslims better – did not venture to remove it. The battle of Roncesvaux
was fought on 15 August 778.

42

Domingo era de Ramos
la Pasión quieren decir,
cuando moros y cristianos
todos entran en la lid.
Ya desmayan los franceses,   5
ya comienzan de huir.
¡Oh cuán bien los esforzaba
ese Roldán paladín!:
'¡Vuelta, vuelta, los franceses
con corazón a la lid!   10
¡Más vale morir por buenos
que deshonrados vivir!'
Ya volvían los franceses
con corazón a la lid;
a los encuentros primeros   15
mataron sesenta mil.
Por las sierras de Altamira
huyendo va el rey Marsín,
caballero en una cebra
no por mengua de rocín;   20
la sangre que dél corría
las yerbas hace teñir;
las voces que iba dando
al cielo quieren subir:
'¡Reniego de ti, Mahoma,   25
y de cuanto hice en ti!
Hícete cuerpo de plata,
pies y manos de un marfil;
hícete casa de Meca
donde adorasen en ti,   30
y por más te honrar, Mahoma,

cabeza de oro te fiz.
Sesenta mil caballeros
a ti te los ofrecí,
mi mujer la reina mora   35
te ofreció treinta mil.'

TEXT: *Prim.* No. 183, from *Canc. de Rom. 'sin año'* (c. 1548).

REFERENCE: Wright, *CG*, 60-2 (but *cebra* in line 79 of the previous ballad and 19 of this is 'wild ass, onager', not 'zebra' as Wright has it).

NOTES: This text is included in order to allow a direct comparison to be drawn between the brief, more highly evolved ballad and the fuller narration (notionally closer to that of the epic) which No. 41 represents. Both versions are attractive in different ways. The short ballad seems to have preserved with a sound instinct the best lines of the longer version. The *novelización* process is apparent in the date ('Domingo de Ramos') and the place ('sierras de Altamira') attributed to the action.

43

En los campos de Alventosa
mataron a don Beltrán,
nunca lo echaron menos
hasta los puertos pasar.
Siete veces echan suertes   5
quién lo volverá a buscar,
todas siete le cupieron
al buen viejo de su padre;
las tres fueron por malicia,
y las cuatro con maldad.   10
    Vuelve riendas al caballo
y vuélveselo a buscar,
de noche por el camino
de día por el jaral.
Por la matanza va el viejo,   15
por la matanza adelante;
los brazos lleva cansados
de los muertos rodear;
no hallaba al que busca,
ni menos la su señal;   20
vido todos los franceses
y no vido a don Beltrán.
Maldiciendo iba el vino,
maldiciendo iba el pan

(el que comían los moros,   25
que no el de la cristiandad),
maldiciendo iba el árbol
que solo en el campo nace,
que todas las aves del cielo
allí se vienen a asentar,   30
que de rama ni de hoja
no la dejaban gozar;
maldiciendo iba al caballero
que cabalgaba sin paje;
si se le cae la lanza   35
no tiene quien se la alce,
y si se le cae la espuela
no tiene quien se la calce;
maldiciendo iba la mujer
que tan sólo un hijo pare: 40
si enemigos se lo matan
no tiene quien lo vengar.
　A la entrada de un puerto
saliendo de un arenal,
vio en esto estar un moro   45
que velaba en un adarve;
hablóle en algarabía
como aquel que bien la sabe:
'Por Dios te ruego, el moro,
me digas una verdad: 50
caballero de armas blancas
si lo viste acá pasar,
y si tú lo tienes preso
a oro te lo pesarán,
y si tú lo tienes muerto   55
désmelo para enterrar,
pues que el cuerpo sin el alma
sólo un dinero no vale.'
　'Ese caballero, amigo,
dime tú qué señas trae.'   60
　'Blancas armas son las suyas
y el caballo es alazán,
y en el carrillo derecho
él tenía una señal
que siendo niño pequeño   65
se la hizo un gavilán.'
　'Ese caballero, amigo,

muerto está en aquel pradal;
las piernas tiene en el agua
y el cuerpo en el arenal;   70
siete lanzadas tenía
desde el hombro al carcañal,
y otras tantas su caballo
desde la cincha al pretal.
No le des culpa al caballo,   75
que no se la puedes dar;
que siete veces lo sacó
sin herida y sin señal,
y otras tantas lo volvió
con gana de pelear.'   80

TEXT: *Prim.* No. 185a, from *Canc. de Rom.* of 1550.

REFERENCES: *Tratado* II, 371-3; *Rom. hisp.* I, 165-6; J. Horrent, *La Chanson de Roland...*, 508-17; Wright, *CG*, 62-3.

NOTES: Menéndez y Pelayo observes that no 'Beltrán' figures in any known version of the *Chanson de Roland*, but that this episode may have been suggested by the passage in that poem (lines 2185 ff. of the 'Oxford' MS) in which Roland, in a lull in the fighting, lifts his dead comrades so that they may receive Archbishop Turpin's blessing. The ballad is in no way inferior to this part of the French text in its pathos. The ballad was preserved in the oral tradition of Galicia and Portugal.

44

En París está doña Alda
la esposa de don Roldán,
trescientas damas con ella
para la acompañar;
todas visten un vestido,   5
todas calzan un calzar,
todas comen a una mesa,
todas comían de un pan,
si no era doña Alda
que era la mayoral.   10
Las ciento hilaban oro,
las ciento tejen cendal,
las ciento tañen instrumentos
para doña Alda holgar.
Al son de los instrumentos   15
doña Alda adormido se ha;

ensoñado había un sueño,
un sueño de gran pesar.
Recordó despavorida
y con un pavor muy grande,   20
los gritos daba tan grandes
que se oían en la ciudad.
Allí hablaron sus doncellas,
bien oiréis lo que dirán:
'¿Qué es aquesto, mi señora?   25
¿Quién es el que os hizo mal?'
'Un sueño soñé, doncellas,
que me ha dado gran pesar:
que me veía en un monte
en un desierto lugar;   30
de so los montes muy altos
un azor vide volar,
tras dél viene una aguililla
que lo ahínca muy mal.
El azor con grande cuita   35
metióse so mi brial;
el aguililla con grande ira
de allí lo iba a sacar;
con las uñas lo despluma,
con el pico lo deshace.'   40
    Allí habló su camarera,
bien oiréis lo que dirá:
'Aquese sueño, señora,
bien os lo entiendo soltar:
el azor es vuestro esposo   45
que viene de allén la mar;
el águila sodes vos
con la cual ha de casar,
y aquel monte es la iglesia
donde os han de velar.'   50
'Si así es, mi camarera,
bien te lo entiendo pagar.'
    Otro día de mañana
cartas de fuera le traen;
tintas venían de dentro,   55
de fuera escritas con sangre,
que su Roldán era muerto
en la caza de Roncesvalles.

82

II: Carolingian Ballads

TEXT: *Prim.* No. 184, from *Canc. de Rom.* of 1550.

TRANSLATIONS: Lockhart No. 41, 'Lady Alda's Dream'; Gibson p. 324; Wright No. 16.

REFERENCES: *Tratado* II, 368-71; *Rom. hisp.* I, 249-51, 266; J. Horrent, *La Chanson de Roland...*, 517-21; C. Segre, 'Il sogno di Alda tra "chanson de geste", "chanson de femme" e "romance" ', *Medioevo Romanzo* 8 (1981-83) 3-9; Wright, *CG*, 63-4.

NOTES: The taste of the centuries and of poets and translators in many lands has surely not erred in declaring this one of the finest of the ballads. It is notable not only for its pathos but for the way in which – as is infrequent in the ballads – it sets out to create a scene for the visual delectation of the listener; and there is not a weak line in it. 'La belle Aude', Roland's betrothed, has only a small place in the earliest ('Oxford') version of the *Chanson de Roland*: Charlemagne brings her the news of Roland's death in the space of one laisse. In a late 12th-century version of the *Chanson* this scene is expanded to 34 laisses, 5 of which recount a completely new epi- sode, Aude's prophetic dream. This version or a similar one then passed into the Spanish *Roncesvalles* adaptation, from which the ballad derives. Menéndez Pidal insists on the superiority of the brief, plain ballad over the diffuse and melodramatic French epic text, and notes that the ballad is strongly represented in the oral tradition of the Jews of N. Africa and the Near East.

45

Por los caños de Carmona
por do va el agua a Sevilla,
por ahí iba Valdovinos
y con él su linda amiga.
Los pies lleva por el agua   5
y la mano en la loriga,
con el temor de los moros
no le tuviesen espía.
Júntanse boca con boca,
nadie no los impedía.   10
Valdovinos con angustia
un suspiro dado había:
'¿Por qué suspiráis, señor,
corazón y vida mía?
O tenéis miedo a los moros   15
o en Francia tenéis amiga.'
'No tengo miedo a los moros
ni en Francia tengo amiga;
mas vos, mora, y yo cristiano

83

hacemos muy mala vida: 20
comemos la carne en viernes
lo que mi ley defendía.
Siete años había, siete,
que yo misa no oía;
si el emperador lo sabe   25
la vida me costaría.'
'Por tus amores, Valdovinos,
cristiana me tornaría.'
'Yo, señora, por los vuestros,
moro de la morería.'   30

TEXT: *Prim.* No. 51 of Menéndez Pelayo's *Apéndice* I, from a collection
of ballads published by Juan de Ribera in 1605.

REFERENCES: *Tratado* II, 391-3; R. Menéndez Pidal, 'La *Chanson des
Saisnes* en España', *Mélanges de Linguistique et de Littérature Romanes
offerts à Mario Roques* (Paris: Bade, 1950), I, 229-44, and *Rom. hisp.* I,
251-3; Wright, *CG*, 64-5.

NOTES: It is curious to note that in a version of this ballad printed in the
Canc. de Rom. 'sin año' (c. 1548), the last two lines were omitted: the
Moorish girl still offers to convert, but not Valdovinos. The latter is
Baudoins (Baldwin) in French, and the ballad derives – somewhat re-
motely – from the French epic *Chanson des Saisnes* (i.e. Saxons, in
Germany) composed about 1200 by Jean Bodel.

46

'Nuño Vero, Nuño Vero,
buen caballero probado,
hinquedes la lanza en tierra
y arrendedes el caballo;
preguntaros he por nuevas   5
de Valdovinos el franco.'
'Aquesas nuevas, señora,
yo vos las diré de grado:
esta noche a medianoche
entramos en cabalgada,   10
y los muchos a los pocos
lleváronnos de arrancada;
hirieron a Valdovinos
de una mala lanzada,
la lanza tenía dentro,   15
de fuera le tiembla el asta;

o esta noche morirá
o de buena madrugada.
Si te pluguiese, Sebilla,
fueses tú mi enamorada.'   20
    'Nuño Vero, Nuño Vero,
mal caballero probado,
yo te pregunto por nuevas,
tu respóndesme al contrario;
que aquesta noche pasada   25
conmigo durmió el franco;
él me diera una sortija
y yo le di un pendón labrado.'

TEXT: *Prim.* No. 168, from *Canc. de Rom. 'sin año'* (c. 1548).

REFERENCES: *Tratado* II, 391-3; *Rom. hisp.* I, 251-3.

NOTES: This ballad also derives indirectly from Bodel's *Chanson des Saisnes* (laisses 137-44). It is a model of ballad compression and a fine example of how names and situations are altered as a legend evolves. The *Chanson des Saisnes* dealt with the Emperor's campaign against the pagan Saxons along the Rhine; in it, Baudoin swam the river to join his mistress, the pagan queen Sébilie, and it was Justamont, Saracen emperor of Persia, who brought the false report of Baudoin's death. In the previous ballad (No. 45) the action has moved from the Rhine to Seville because of the suggestion of the name Sébilie, and the river has become the 'caños' or aqueduct from Carmona; and in this ballad Justamont has become Nuño Vero. Menéndez Pidal postulated the existence of a lost *Cantar de Sansueña* (i.e., Saxony) as an intermediary between the French epic and the Spanish ballads.

47

    Del Soldán de Babilonia
de ése os quiero decir,
que le dé Dios mala vida
y a la postre peor fin.
Armó naves y galeras,   5
pasan de sesenta mil,
para ir a combatir
a Narbona la gentil.
Allá van a echar áncoras
allá al puerto de San Gil,   10
cautivado han al conde
al conde Benalmenique:
desciéndenlo de una torre,

cabálganlo en un rocín,
la cola le dan por riendas   15
por más deshonrado ir.
Cien azotes dan al conde
y otros tantos al rocín,
al rocín porque anduviese
y al conde por lo rendir.   20
    La condesa desque lo supo
sáleselo a recibir:
'Pésame de vos, señor,
conde, de veros así,
daré yo por vos, el conde,   25
las doblas sesenta mil,
y si no bastaren, conde,
a Narbona la gentil.
Si esto no bastare, el conde,
a tres hijas que yo parí;   30
yo las pariera, buen conde,
y vos las hubiste en mí;
y si no bastare, conde,
señor, védesme aquí a mí.'
'Muchas mercedes, condesa,   35
por vuestro tan buen decir;
no dedes por mí, señora,
tan sólo un maravedí;
heridas tengo de muerte,
de ellas no puedo guarir;   40
¡adiós, adiós, la condesa,
que ya me mandan ir de aquí!'
    'Vayades con Dios, el conde,
y con la gracia de San Gil;
Dios os lo eche en suerte   45
a ese Roldán paladín.'

TEXT: *Prim.* No. 196, from *Canc. de Rom.* of 1550.

REFERENCES: *Tratado* II, 408-10; *Rom. hisp.* I, 258-9.

NOTES: This ballad summarises the action of the first part of the French epic *La Mort d'Aimeri de Narbonne*, a late 12th-century poem with a setting in Provence. In its Spanish form the count's name, Benalmenique, seems closer to Occitan *n'Aimeric* than to French. The heroic offers of the countess are not present in the French poem; Menéndez Pidal supposed a free Spanish translation of the epic as an intermediary.

48

En Castilla está un castillo
que se llama Rocafrida;
al castillo llaman Roca
y a la fonte llaman Frida.
El pie tenía de oro   5
y almenas de plata fina;
entre almena y almena
está una piedra zafira,
tanto relumbra de noche
como el sol a mediodía.   10
Dentro estaba una doncella
que llaman Rosaflorida;
siete condes la demandan,
tres duques de Lombardía;
a todos los desdeñaba   15
tanta es su lozanía.
Enamoróse de Montesinos
de oídas, que no de vista.
Una noche estando así
gritos da Rosaflorida: 20
oyérala un camarero
que en su cámara dormía:
'¿Qué es aquesto, mi señora?
¿Qué es esto, Rosaflorida?
O tenedes mal de amores   25
o estáis loca sandía.'
'Ni yo tengo mal de amores
ni estoy loca sandía;
mas llevásesme estas cartas
a Francia la bien guarnida,   30
diéseslas a Montesinos,
la cosa que yo más quería;
dile que me venga ver
para la Pascua Florida;
darle he yo este mi cuerpo   35
el más lindo que hay en Castilla,
si no es el de mi hermana
que de fuego sea ardida;
y si de mí más quisiere
yo mucho más le daría: 40
darle he siete castillos
los mejores que hay en Castilla.'

TEXT: *Prim.* No. 179, from *Canc. de Rom. 'sin año'* (c. 1548).

TRANSLATIONS: Gibson p. 319; Wright No. 17.

REFERENCES: *Tratado* II, 411-15; *Rom. hisp.* I, 259-61; Wright, *CG*, 66.

NOTES: This enchanting ballad derives from some late version of the French epic *Aïol* (c. 1200). The hero Aïols ('serpents') has his original name in its Spanish form 'Ayuelos' in the next ballad, but in this one as in many others he is called 'Montesinos' ('pues nació en ásperos montes', says Menéndez Pidal). An older and much less highly evolved version of the text is given in the MS *Cancionero de Londres* and is there attributed to Juan Rodríguez del Padrón who was writing about 1430-40. It has been recorded from the oral tradition in Catalonia and among the Jews of Morocco. In Philip II's day the legend had associations with a spot near Montiel on the Guadiana (province of Ciudad Real), where were the ruins of the Rocafrida castle, a spring called the Fontefrida, and not far away the famous Cueva de Montesinos. The ruins of the Visigothic settlement of Recópolis, later Racúpel, in Guadalajara province, were also claimed to be those of Rosaflorida's castle. The place-names *Rocafrida*, *Fontefrida* have an archaic flavour and are possibly (like *Montiel*) of the Mozarabic dialect.

49

Todas las gentes dormían
(en las que Dios tiene parte),
mas no duerme Melisenda
la hija del emperante,
que amores del conde Ayuelos   5
no la dejan reposar.
Salto diera de la cama
como la parió su madre,
vistiérase una alcandora
no hallando su brial;   10
vase para los palacios
donde sus damas están,
dando palmadas en ellas
las empezó de llamar:
'Si dormís, las mis doncellas,   15
si dormides, recordad;
las que sabedes de amores
consejo me queráis dar,
las que de amores no sabedes
tengádesme poridad: 20

amores del conde Ayuelos
no me dejan reposar.'
Allí hablara una vieja,
vieja es de antigua edad:
'Agora es tiempo, señora,   25
de los placeres tomar,
que si esperáis a vejez
no vos querrá un rapaz.'
Desque esto oyó Melisenda
no quiso más esperar,   30
y vase a buscar al conde
a los palacios do está.
Topara con Hernandillo
un alguacil de su padre:
'¿Qué es aquesto, Melisenda?   35
Esto ¿qué podía estar?
¡O vos tenedes mal de amores
o os queréis loca tornar!'
'Que no tengo mal de amores
ni tengo por quién penar,   40
mas cuando yo era pequeña
tuve una enfermedad;
prometí tener novenas
allá en San Juan de Letrán;
las dueñas iban de día,   45
doncellas agora van.'
Desque esto oyera Hernando
puso fin a su hablar;
la infanta, mal enojada,
queriendo dél se vengar: 50
'Prestásesme', dijo a Hernando,
'prestásesme tu puñal,
que miedo me tengo, miedo,
de los perros de la calle.'
Tomó el puñal por la punta,   55
los cabos le fue a dar;
diérale tal puñalada
que en el suelo muerto cae,
y vase para el palacio
ado el conde Ayuelos está.   60
    Las puertas halló cerradas,
no sabe por dó entrar;
con arte de encantamiento

las abrió de par en par.
Al estruendo el conde Ayuelos   65
empezara de llamar:
'¡Socorred, mis caballeros,
socorred sin más tardar;
creo son mis enemigos
que me vienen a matar!'   70
La Melisenda discreta
le empezara de hablar:
'No te congojes, señor,
no quieras pavor tomar,
que yo soy una morica   75
venida de allende el mar.'
Desque esto oyera el conde
luego conocido la ha;
fuese el conde para ella,
las manos le fue a tomar,   80
y a la sombra de un laurel
de Venus es su jugar.

TEXT: *Prim.* No. 198, from a *pliego suelto* of the 16th century.

TRANSLATION: Wright No. 18.

REFERENCES: *Tratado* II, 388-91; *Rom. hisp.* I, 261; Wright, *CG*, 66-7.

NOTES: This sort of adventure is found in several of the French epics. From the personal names of the ballad it seems to derive ultimately from two of them, *Amis et Amile* and *Aïol*. The ballad has been recorded from the oral tradition of the Jews of N. Africa and the Balkans.

50

Estábase la condesa
en su estrado asentada,
tijericas de oro en la mano
su hijo afeitando estaba;
palabras le está diciendo   5
palabras de gran pesar;
las palabras eran tales
que al niño hacen llorar:
'Dios te dé barbas en rostro
y te haga barragán;   10
déte Dios ventura en armas
como el paladín Roldán,
porque vengases, mi hijo,

la muerte de vuestro padre;
matáronlo a traición
por casar con vuestra madre.
Ricas bodas me hicieron
en las cuales Dios no ha parte,
ricos paños me cortaron
la reina no los ha tales.'
    Maguera pequeño el niño
bien entendido la ha.
Allí respondió Gaiferos,
bien oiréis lo que dirá:
'Así ruego a Dios del cielo
y a Santa María su madre.'
    Oídolo había el conde
en los palacios do está:
'¡Calles, calles, la condesa,
boca mala sin verdad!
Que yo no matara al conde
ni le hiciera matar;
mas tus palabras, condesa,
el niño me las pagará.'
Mandó llamar escuderos,
criados son de su padre,
para que lleven al niño
que lo lleven a matar.
La muerte que él les dijera
mancilla es de la escuchar:
'Córtenle el pie del estribo,
la mano del gavilán,
sáquenle ambos los ojos
por más seguro andar;
y el dedo, y el corazón
traédmelo por señal.'
    Ya lo llevan a Gaiferos,
ya lo llevan a matar.
Hablaban los escuderos
con mancilla que dél han:
'¡Oh válasme Dios del cielo
y Santa María su madre!
Si este niño matamos
¿qué galardón nos darán?'
Ellos en aquesto estando
no sabiendo qué harán,

15

20

25

30

35

40

45

50

55

vieron venir una perrita
de la condesa su madre.
Allí habló uno de ellos,
bien oiréis lo que dirá: 60
'Matemos esta perrita
por nuestra seguridad,
saquémosle el corazón
y llevémoslo a Galván,
cortémosle el dedo al chico 65
por llevar mejor señal.'
Ya tomaban a Gaiferos
para el dedo le cortar:
'Venid acá vos, Gaiferos,
y querednos escuchar; 70
vos íos de aquesta tierra
y en ella no parezcáis más.'
Ya le daban entre señas
el camino que hará:
'Irvos heis de tierra en tierra 75
a do vuestro tío está.'
Gaiferos desconsolado
por ese mundo se va;
los escuderos se volvieron
para do estaba Galván. 80
Danle el dedo, y el corazón,
y dicen que muerto lo han.
La condesa que esto oyera
empezara gritos dar;
lloraba de los sus ojos 85
que quería reventar.
Dejemos a la condesa
que muy grande llanto hace,
y digamos de Gaiferos
del camino por do va, 90
que de día ni de noche
no hace sino caminar,
hasta que llegó a la tierra
adonde su tío está.
Dícele de esta manera 95
y empezóle de hablar:
'Manténgaos Dios, el mi tío.'
'Mi sobrino, bien vengáis.
¿Qué buena venida es ésta?

Vos me la queráis contar.'   100
'La venida que yo tengo
triste es y con pesar,
que Galván con grande enojo
mandado me había matar;
mas lo que vos ruego, mi tío,   105
y lo que vos vengo a rogar,
vamos a vengar la muerte
de vuestro hermano, mi padre;
matáronlo a traición
por casar con la mi madre.'   110
'Sosegaos, el mi sobrino,
vos queráis asosegar,
que la muerte de mi hermano
bien la iremos a vengar.'
    Y ellos así estuvieron   115
dos años y aun más,
hasta que dijo Gaiferos
y empezara de hablar:...

TEXT: *Prim.* No. 171, from *Canc. de Rom. 'sin año'* (c. 1548).

REFERENCES: *Tratado* II, 378-83; *Rom. hisp.* I, 273-4; (on the legend) P. Dronke, 'Waltharius-Gaiferos', ch. 2 of *Barbara et antiquissima carmina* (Barcelona: Universidad Autónoma, 1977); Wright, *CG*, 67-8.

NOTES: This, like the Carolingian ballads which follow, is a *juglaresco* text, lively enough in its fashion although still containing a large number of features which the *autor-legión* would not have tolerated. Menéndez Pidal observes, however, that this and the following ballad have become traditional in some parts in versions which unite the two and then reduce their length to about half, a case (by no means unique) of poems which have become traditional only after being printed in the 16th century. Gaiferos is *Gaifiers* in French legend; in history he was *Waifre* or *Waifarius*, Duke of Aquitania, killed in 769.

51

'Vámonos', dijo, 'mi tío,
a París esa ciudad,
en figura de romeros
no nos conozca Galván:
que si Galván nos conoce   5
mandar nos hía matar.
Encima ropas de seda

vistamos las de sayal,
llevemos nuestras espadas
por más seguros andar;   10
llevemos sendos bordones
por la gente asegurar.'
Ya se parten los romeros,
ya se parten, ya se van,
de noche por los caminos   15
de día por los jarales.
  Andando por sus jornadas
a París llegado han;
las puertas hallan cerradas,
no hallan por donde entrar,   20
siete vueltas la rodean
por ver si podrán entrar,
y al cabo de las ocho
un postigo van hallar.
Ellos que se vieron dentro   25
empiezan a demandar;
no preguntan por mesón
ni menos por hospital,
preguntan por los palacios
donde la condesa está;   30
a las puertas del palacio
allí van a demandar.
Vieron estar la condesa
y empezaron de hablar:
'Dios te salve, la condesa.'   35
'Los romeros, bien vengáis.'
'Mandedes nos dar limosna
por honor de caridad.'
'Con Dios vades, los romeros,
que no os puedo nada dar,   40
que el conde me había mandado
a romeros no albergar.'
'Dadnos limosna, señora,
que el conde no lo sabrá;
así la den a Gaiferos   45
en la tierra donde está.'
Así como oyó *Gaiferos*
comenzó de suspirar:
mandábales dar del vino,
mandábales dar del pan.   50

Ellos en aquesto estando
el conde llegado ha:
'¿Qué es aquesto, la condesa?
aquesto ¿qué puede estar?
¿No os tenía ya mandado   55
a romeros no albergar?'
Y alzara la su mano,
puñada le fuera a dar,
que sus dientes menudicos
en tierra los fuera a echar.   60
Allí hablaron los romeros
y empiezan de hablar:
'¡Por hacer bien la condesa
cierto no merece mal!'
'¡Calledes vos, los romeros,   65
no hayades vuestra parte!'
Alzó Gaiferos su espada,
un golpe le fue a dar
que la cabeza de sus hombros
en tierra la fuera a echar.   70
Allí habló la condesa
llorando con gran pesar:
'¿Quién érades, los romeros,
que al conde fuistes matar?'
Allí respondió el romero,   75
tal respuesta le fue a dar:
'Yo soy Gaiferos, señora,
vuestro hijo natural.'
'Aquesto no puede ser
ni era cosa de verdad,   80
que el dedo, y el corazón
yo lo tengo por señal.'
'El corazón que vos tenéis
en persona no fue a estar,
el dedo bien es aquéste   85
que en esta mano me falta.'
La condesa que esto oyera
empezóle de abrazar;
la tristeza que tenía
en placer se fue a tornar.   90

TEXT: *Prim.* No. 172, from *Canc. de Rom. 'sin año'* (c. 1548).

REFERENCES: *Tratado* II, 383-4; *Rom. hisp.* I, 273-4.

NOTES: The popularity of this and the previous ballad in the Golden Age
and in the modern oral tradition is evidenced by the fact that the fourth
line became proverbial. Menéndez Pidal says: 'Todo lo desfigurado, lo
difícil de conocer, se expresaba con el verso *no lo conozca Galván, no lo
conocerá Galván'*, and similar expressions are still registered in modern
dictionaries.

52

'Durandarte, Durandarte,
buen caballero probado,
yo te ruego que hablemos
en aquel tiempo pasado,
y dime si se te acuerda   5
cuando fuiste enamorado,
cuando en galas e invenciones
publicabas tu cuidado,
cuando venciste a los moros
en campo por mí aplazado;   10
agora, desconocido,
di ¿por qué me has olvidado?'
        'Palabras son lisonjeras,
señora, de vuestro grado,
que si yo mudanza hice   15
vos lo habéis todo causado,
pues amastes a Gaiferos
cuando yo fui desterrado;
que si amor queréis conmigo
tenéislo muy mal pensado,   20
que por no sufrir ultraje
moriré desesperado.'

TEXT: *Prim.* No. 180, from *Canc. de Rom. 'sin año'* (c. 1548).

REFERENCE: *Tratado* I, 423-4.

NOTES: The transformation of Roland's sword *Durandel* into a knight
killed at Roncesvaux (in the next ballad) had already taken place in one of
the latest French epics. His further evolution into a symbol of constancy
in love sems to be purely Spanish and more in keeping with the world of
Amadís de Gaula than with that of Carolingian heroes. The ballad was
included in two *cancioneros* of the early 16th century and was a favourite
during the Golden Age.

53

'¡Oh Belerma!, ¡oh Belerma!
por mi mal fuiste engendrada,
que siete años te serví
sin de ti alcanzar nada;
agora que me querías   5
muero yo en esta batalla.
No me pesa de mi muerte
aunque temprano me llama,
más pésame que de verte
y de servirte dejaba.   10
¡Oh mi primo Montesinos!
lo que agora yo os rogaba,
que cuando yo fuere muerto
y mi ánima arrancada,
vos llevéis mi corazón   15
adonde Belerma estaba,
y servidla de mi parte
como de vos yo esperaba,
y traedle a la memoria
dos veces cada semana,   20
y diréisle que se acuerde
cuán cara que me costaba;
y dadle todas mis tierras
las que yo señoreaba,
pues que yo a ella pierdo   25
todo el bien con ella vaya.
¡Montesinos, Montesinos!
¡mal me aqueja esta lanzada!
el brazo traigo cansado
y la mano de la espada;   30
traigo grandes las heridas,
mucha sangre derramada,
los extremos tengo fríos
y el corazón me desmaya;
que ojos que nos vieron ir   35
nunca nos verán en Francia.
Abracéisme, Montesinos,
que ya se me sale el alma;
de mis ojos ya no veo,
la lengua tengo turbada;   40
yo vos doy todos mis cargos

en vos yo los traspasaba.'
'El Señor en quien creéis
Él oiga vuestra palabra.'
   Muerto yace Durandarte   45
al pie de una alta montaña,
llorábalo Montesinos
que a su muerte se hallara;
quitándole está el almete,
desciñéndole la espada;   50
hácele la sepultura
con una pequeña daga;
sacábale el corazón
como él se lo jurara,
para llevar a Belerma   55
como él se lo mandara.
Las palabras que le dice
de allá le salen del alma:
'¡Oh mi primo Durandarte!
¡Primo mío de mi alma!   60
¡Espada nunca vencida!
¡Esfuerzo do esfuerzo estaba!
¡Quien a vos mató, mi primo,
no sé por qué me dejara!'

TEXT: *Prim.* No. 181, from *Canc. de Rom. 'sin año'* (c. 1548).

TRANSLATION: Gibson p. 321.

REFERENCES: *Tratado* II, 423-5; Wright, *CG*, 68.

NOTES: The transformation of the material of this ballad into the extraordinary invention of Don Quixote's adventure in the *Cueva de Montesinos* (II, 22 & 23) has been mentioned in the Introduction. This is perhaps the most striking example of the power of suggestion which the brief, plain ballad text can exercise upon an imaginative mind. Góngora in 1582 wrote a sort of response to, and continuation of the tale as a parody of the Carolingian genre:

       Diez años vivió Belerma
       con el corazón difunto
       que le dejó en testamento
       aquel francés boquirrubio...

which is a masterpiece of its kind. On this, and on Cervantes' reaction to it in *Don Quixote*, see J. Gornall & C. Smith, 'Góngora, Cervantes, and the *Romancero*: Some Interactions', *Modern Language Review* 80 (1985) 351-61.

54

Medianoche era por filo
los gallos querían cantar,
conde Claros con amores
no podía reposar;
dando muy grandes suspiros   5
que el amor le hacía dar,
porque amor de Claraniña
no le deja sosegar.
Cuando vino la mañana
que quería alborear,   10
salto diera de la cama
que parece un gavilán;
voces da por el palacio
y empezara de llamar:
'Levantad, mi camarero,   15
dadme vestir y calzar.'
    Presto estaba el camarero
para habérselo de dar:
diérale calzas de grana,
borceguíes de cordobán,   20
diérale jubón de seda
aforrado en zarzahán,
diérale un manto rico
que no se puede apreciar,
trescientas piedras preciosas   25
al derredor del collar;
tráele un rico caballo
que en la corte no hay su par,
que la silla con el freno
bien valía una ciudad,   30
con trescientos cascabeles
alrededor del petral,
los ciento eran de oro
y los ciento de metal,
y los ciento son de plata   35
por los sones concordar;
y vase para el palacio
para el palacio real.
A la infanta Claraniña
allí la fuera hallar,   40
trescientas damas con ella

que la van acompañar.
Tan linda va Claraniña
que a todos hace penar.
   Conde Claros que la vido   45
luego va descabalgar,
las rodillas por el suelo
le comenzó de hablar:
'Mantenga Dios a tu Alteza.'
'Conde Claros, bien vengáis.'   50
Las palabras que prosigue
eran para enamorar:
'Conde Claros, Conde Claros,
el señor de Montalván,
¡cómo habéis hermoso cuerpo   55
para con moros lidiar!'
Respondiera el conde Claros,
tal respuesta le fue a dar:
'Mi cuerpo tengo, señora,
para con damas holgar;   60
si yo os tuviese esta noche
señora, a mi mandar,
otro día en la mañana
con cien moros pelear,
si a todos no los venciese   65
que me mandasen matar.'
'Calledes, conde, calledes,
y no os queráis alabar;
el que quiere servir damas
así lo suele hablar,   70
y al entrar en las batallas
bien se saben excusar.'
'Si no lo creéis, señora,
por las obras se verá;
siete años son pasados   75
que os empecé de amar,
que de noche yo no duermo
ni de día puedo holgar.'
'Siempre os preciastes, conde,
de las damas os burlar;   80
mas déjame ir a los baños,
a los baños a bañar;
cuando yo sea bañada
estoy a vuestro mandar.'

Respondiérale el buen conde,   85
tal respuesta le fue a dar:
'Bien sabedes vos, señora,
que soy cazador real;
caza que tengo en la mano
nunca la puedo dejar.'   90
Tomárala por la mano,
para un vergel se van;
a la sombra de un ciprés
debajo de un rosal
de la cintura arriba   95
tan dulces besos se dan,
de la cintura abajo
como hombre y mujer se han.
   Mas la fortuna adversa
que a placeres da pesar,   100
por ahí pasó un cazador
que no debía de pasar,
detrás de una podenca
que rabia debía matar;
vido estar al conde Claros   105
con la infanta a bel holgar.
El conde cuando le vido
empezóle de llamar:
'Ven acá tú, el cazador,
así Dios te guarde de mal;   110
de todo lo que has visto
tú nos tengas poridad.
Darte he yo mil marcos de oro
y si más quisieres, más;
casarte he con una doncella   115
que era mi prima carnal;
darte he en arras y en dote
la villa de Montalván;
de otra parte la infanta
mucho más te puede dar.'   120
   El cazador sin ventura
no les quiso escuchar;
vase para los palacios
ado el buen rey está:
'Manténgate Dios, el rey,   125
y a tu corona real;
una nueva yo te traigo

dolorosa y de pesar,
que no os cumple traer corona
ni en caballo cabalgar,   130
la corona de la cabeza
bien la podéis vos quitar,
si tal deshonra como ésta
la hubiéseis de comportar.
Que he hallado la infanta   135
con Claros de Montalván
besándola y abrazando
en vuestro huerto real;
de la cintura abajo
como hombre y mujer se han.'   140
    El rey con muy grande enojo
al cazador mandó matar,
porque había sido osado
de tales nuevas llevar.
Mandó llamar sus alguaciles   145
aprisa, no de vagar,
mandó armar quinientos hombres
que le hayan de acompañar
para que prendan al conde
y le hayan de tomar,   150
y mandó cerrar las puertas,
las puertas de la ciudad.
A las puertas del palacio
allá le fueron a hallar;
preso llevan al buen conde   155
con mucha seguridad,
unos grillos a los pies
que bien pesan un quintal,
las esposas a las manos
que era dolor de mirar,   160
una cadena a su cuello
que de hierro era el collar;
cabálganle en una mula
por más deshonra le dar;
metiéronle en una torre   165
de muy gran oscuridad;
las llaves de la prisión
el rey las quiso llevar,
porque sin licencia suya
nadie le pueda hablar.   170

Por él rogaban los grandes
cuantos en la corte están,
por el rogaba Oliveros,
por el rogaba Roldán,
y ruegan los doce pares   175
de Francia la natural,
y las monjas de Santa Ana
con las de la Trinidad
llevaban un crucifijo
para el buen rey rogar.   180
Con ellas va un arzobispo
y un perlado y cardenal;
mas el rey con grande enojo
a nadie quiso escuchar;
antes de muy enojado   185
sus grandes mandó llamar.
Cuando ya los tuvo juntos
empezóles de hablar:
'Amigos e hijos míos,
a lo que vos hice llamar: 190
ya sabéis que el conde Claros
el señor de Montalván
de cómo le he criado
hasta ponerlo en edad,
y le he guardado su tierra   195
que su padre le fue a dar
(el que morir no debiera,
Reinaldos de Montalván)
y por hacerle yo más grande
de lo mío le quise dar,   200
hícele gobernador
de mi reino natural.
El, por darme galardón,
mirad en que fue a tocar:
que quiso forzar la infanta   205
hija mía natural;
hombre que lo tal comete
¿qué sentencia le han de dar?'
Todos dicen a una voz
que lo hayan de degollar,   210
y así la sentencia dada
el buen rey la fue a firmar.
El arzobispo que esto viera

103

al buen rey fue a hablar,
pidiéndole por merced 215
licencia le quiera dar
para ir a ver al conde
y su muerte le denunciar.
'Pláceme', dijo el buen rey,
'Pláceme de voluntad; 220
mas con esta condición:
que solo habéis de andar
con aqueste pajecico
de quien puedo bien fiar.'
Ya se parte el arzobispo 225
y a las cárceles se va.
Las guardas desque lo vieron
luego le dejan entrar;
con él iba el pajecico
que le va a acompañar. 230
Cuando vido estar al conde
en su prisión y pesar,
las palabras que le dice
dolor eran de escuchar:
'Pésame de vos, el conde, 235
cuanto me puede pesar,
que los yerros por amores
dignos son de perdonar.
Por vos he rogado al rey,
nunca me quiso escuchar; 240
antes ha dado sentencia
que os hayan de degollar.
Yo vos lo dije, sobrino,
que vos dejásedes de amar,
que el que las mujeres ama 245
atal galardón le dan,
que haya de morir por ellas
y en las cárceles penar.'
Respondiera el buen conde
con esfuerzo singular: 250
'¡Calledes, por Dios, mi tío,
no me queráis enojar!
quien no ama las mujeres
no se puede hombre llamar,
mas la vida que yo tengo 255
por ellas quiero gastar.'

Respondió el pajecico,
tal respuesta le fue a dar:
'Conde, bienaventurado
siempre os deben de llamar,   260
porque muerte tan honrada
por vos había de pasar;
más envidia he de vos, conde,
que mancilla ni pesar;
más querría ser vos, conde,   265
que el rey que os manda matar,
porque muerte tan honrada
por mí hubiese de pasar.
Llama yerro la fortuna
quien no la sabe gozar;   270
la prisa del cadahalso
vos, conde, la debéis dar;
si no es dada la sentencia
vos la debéis de firmar.'
El conde que esto oyera   275
tal respuesta le fue a dar:
'Por Dios te ruego, el paje,
en amor de caridad,
que vayas a la princesa
de mi parte a le rogar,   280
que suplico a su Alteza
que ella me salga a mirar,
que en la hora de mi muerte
yo la pueda contemplar,
que si mis ojos la veen   285
mi alma no penará.'
   Ya se parte el pajecico,
ya se parte, ya se va,
llorando de los sus ojos
que quería reventar;   290
topara con la princesa,
bien oiréis lo que dirá:
'Agora es tiempo, señora,
que hayáis a remediar,
que a vuestro querido el conde   295
lo llevan a degollar.'
La infanta, que esto oyera,
en tierra muerta se cae;
damas, dueñas y doncellas

no la pueden retornar, 300
hasta que llegó su aya
la que la fue a criar:
'¿Qué es aquesto, la infanta?
aquesto ¿qué puede estar?'
'¡Ay triste de mí, mezquina, 305
que no sé qué puede estar!
¡Que si al conde me matan
yo me habré desesperar!'
'Saliésedes vos, mi hija,
saliésedes a lo quitar.' 310
    Ya se parte la infanta,
ya se parte, ya se va;
fuese para el mercado
donde lo han de sacar;
vido estar el cadahalso 315
en que lo han de degollar;
damas, dueñas y doncellas
que lo salen a mirar.
Vio venir gente de armas
que lo traen a matar, 320
los pregoneros delante
por su yerro publicar.
Con el poder de la gente
ella no podía pasar:
'Apartadvos, gente de armas, 325
todos me haced lugar,
si no... ¡por vida del rey
a todos mande matar!'
La gente que la conoce
luego le hace lugar, 330
hasta que llegó el conde
y le empezara de hablar:
'Esforzá, esforzá, el buen conde,
y no queráis desmayar,
que aunque yo pierda la vida 335
la vuestra se ha de salvar.'
    El alguacil que esto oyera
comenzó de caminar,
vase para los palacios
adonde el buen rey está: 340
'Cabalgue la vuestra Alteza,
aprisa, no de vagar,

que salida es la infanta
para el conde nos quitar.
Los unos manda que maten,   345
y los otros enhorcar;
si vuestra Alteza no socorre
yo no puedo remediar.'
    El buen rey, de que esto oyera,
comenzó de caminar,   350
y fuese para el mercado
ado el conde fue a hallar:
'¿Qué es esto, la infanta?
aquesto ¿qué puede estar?
La sentencia que yo he dado   355
¿vos la queréis revocar?
Yo juro por mi corona,
por mi corona real,
que si heredero tuviese
que me hubiese de heredar   360
que a vos y al conde Claros
vivos vos haría quemar.'
'Que vos me matéis, mi padre,
muy bien me podéis matar,
mas suplico a vuestra Alteza   365
que se quiera él acordar
de los servicios pasados
de Reinaldos de Montalván,
que murió en las batallas
por tu corona ensalzar;   370
por los servicios del padre
al hijo debes galardonar;
por malquerer de traidores
vos no le debéis matar,
que su muerte será causa   375
que me hayáis de disfamar.
Mas suplico a vuestra Alteza
que se quiera consejar,
que los reyes con furor
no deben de sentenciar,   380
porque el conde es de linaje
del reino más principal,
porque él era de los doce
que a tu mesa comen pan;
sus amigos y parientes   385

todos te querrán mal,
revolver te hían guerra,
tus reinos se perderán.'
El buen rey que esto oyera
comenzara a demandar: 390
'Consejo os pido, los míos,
que me queráis consejar.'
Luego todos se apartaron
por su consejo tomar;
el consejo que le dieron   395
que le haya de perdonar,
por quitar males y bregas
y por la princesa afamar.
Todos firman el perdón,
el buen rey fue a firmar;   400
también le aconsejaron
consejo le fueron dar,
pues la infanta quería al conde
con él haya de casar.
    Ya desfierran al buen conde   405
ya lo mandan desferrar;
descabalga de una mula
el arzobispo a desposar;
él tomóles de las manos,
así los hubo de juntar.   410
Los enojos y pesares
placeres se han de tornar.

TEXT: *Prim.* No. 190, from *Canc. de Rom. 'sin año'* (c. 1548).

TRANSLATION: Wright No. 9 (1).

REFERENCES: *Tratado* II, 399-403; *Rom. hisp.* II, 43-4, 100-1, 186-7; J. Seeger, *Study of an Oral Romance Tradition: The 'Conde Claros de Montalván'* (New York: Garland, 1990); Wright, *CG*, 68-71.

NOTES: This famous ballad recalls, very vaguely, the legend of the love-affair between Charlemagne's daughter Emma and his secretary Egginhard (? Gerineldos, in the next ballad). The legend does not seem to be found in any French text and may have originated in Germany. The ballad was a favourite throughout the Golden Age: it was referred to as something universally known, it contributed a number of lines to the nation's stock of proverbs, and musicians from Juan del Encina onward composed settings for brief sections of it (particularly that beginning at line 235). The opening lines were also commonly used to accompany a courtly dance in the 16th century. Modern oral versions of the ballad are known, especially among the Sephardim. Despite the occasional tediousness of its *juglaresco* formulae and clichés, the ballad is a masterpiece of construction and narration, and Conde Claros, 'un verdadero mártir de amor' (Menéndez y Pelayo), for whom even the nuns prayed, is one of the most attractive figures in the *Romancero*.

55

'Gerineldos, Gerineldos,
mi camarero pulido,
¡quién te tuviera esta noche
tres horas a mi servicio!'
'Como soy vuestro criado,   5
señora, burláis conmigo.'
'No me burlo, Gerineldos,
que de veras te lo digo.'
'¿A cuál hora, bella infanta,
cumpliréis lo prometido?'   10
'Entre la una y las dos
cuando el rey esté dormido.'
Levantóse Gerineldos,
abre en secreto el rastrillo,
calza sandalias de seda   15
para andar sin ser sentido;
tres vueltas le da al palacio
y otras tantas al castillo.
'Abráisme', dijo, 'señora,
abráisme, cuerpo garrido.'   20
'¿Quién sois vos, el caballero,
que llamáis así al postigo?'
'Gerineldos soy, señora,
vuestro tan querido amigo.'
Tomáralo por la mano,   25
a su lecho lo ha subido,
y besando y abrazando
Gerineldos se ha dormido.
Recordado había el rey
del sueño despavorido,   30
tres veces lo había llamado,
ninguna le ha respondido.
'Gerineldos, Gerineldos,
mi camarero pulido,
¿si me andas en traición,   35

trátasme como a enemigo?
O con la infanta dormías
o el alcázar me has vendido.'
Tomó la espada en la mano
con gran saña va encendido,   40
fuérase para la cama
donde a Gerineldos vido.
El quisiéralo matar
mas crióle desde niño.
Sacara luego la espada   45
entre entrambos la ha metido,
para que al volver del sueño
catasen que el yerro han visto.
   Recordado hubo la infanta,
vio la espada y dio un suspiro: 50
'Recordar heis, Gerineldos,
que ya érades sentido;
que la espada de mi padre
de nuestro yerro es testigo.'
Gerineldos va a su estancia,   55
le sale el rey de improviso:
'¿Dónde vienes, Gerineldos,
tan mustio, descolorido?'
'Del jardín vengo, señor,
de coger flores y lirios,   60
y la rosa más fragante
mis colores ha comido.'
'¡Mientes, mientes, Gerineldos,
que con la infanta has dormido;
testigo de ella mi espada,   65
en su filo está el castigo!'

TEXT: Recorded in the late 19th century in Andalusia, and printed by Menéndez y Pelayo among the *Romances populares*, vol. X of the *Antología de poetas líricos*, p. 161.

TRANSLATION: Wright No. 3.

REFERENCES: *Tratado* II, 404-5; R. Menéndez Pidal, 'Sobre geografía folklórica: ensayo de un método', *Revista de Filología Española* 7 (1920) 229-67; D. Catalán & A. Galmés, *Cómo vive un romance: dos ensayos de tradicionalidad* (Madrid: CSIC, 1954) (an extensive revision of Menéndez Pidal's 1920 study); *Rom. hisp.* I, 73; II, 77, 393-401; *Rom. trad.*, VI-VIII; Wright, *CG*, 71-2.

NOTES: A modern oral version chosen from the many that have been recorded from most parts of the Peninsula is here preferred to the two texts printed in the 16th century, both poor ones. This seems to be the best-known ballad among country people in our century; it is certainly that which has been subjected to the most intensive investigation by scholars, in studies which are classics of their kind.

III

NOVELESQUE BALLADS

56

Herido está don Tristán
de una mala lanzada;
diérasela el rey su tío
por celos que dél cataba.
El hierro tiene en el cuerpo,   5
de fuera le tiembla el asta.
Valo a ver la reina Iseo
por la su desdicha mala;
júntanse boca con boca
cuanto una misa rezada,   10
llora el uno, llora el otro,
la cama bañan en agua;
allí nace un arboledo
que azucena se llamaba,
cualquier mujer que la come   15
luego se siente preñada;
comiérala reina Iseo
por la su desdicha mala.

TEXT: *Prim.* No. 146, from *Canc. de Rom. 'sin año'* (c. 1548).

REFERENCES: *Tratado* II, 469-73; B. Pelegrín, 'Flechazo y lanzada, Eros y Tánatos', *Prohemio* 6 (1975) 83-115; Wright, *CG*, 73-4; G. Di Stefano, 'El *Romance de Don Tristán*: Edición "crítica" y comentarios', in *Studia in honorem prof. M. de Riquer* (Barcelona: Quaderns Crema, 1988), III, 271-303.

NOTES: This and the next two texts are almost the only ballad representatives of the prose tales which circulated in the Peninsula during the 14th and 15th centuries on the theme of *Tristram and Isolde*, as translations and free adaptations of the French legends known collectively as the *matière de Bretagne*. The magical properties of the lily seem to be a purely Spanish addition to the legend. In its brevity the ballad probably has claims

to some antiquity; it is said to have been a favourite with the ladies of
Queen Isabel's court.

57

Nunca fuera caballero
de damas tan bien servido
como fuera Lanzarote
cuando de Bretaña vino:
que dueñas curaban dél,   5
doncellas del su rocino,
esa dueña Quintañona
ésa le escanciaba el vino,
la linda reina Ginebra
se lo acostaba consigo;   10
y estando al mejor sabor
que sueño no había dormido,
la reina toda turbada
un pleito ha conmovido:
'Lanzarote, Lanzarote,   15
si antes hubieras venido
no hablara el orgulloso
las palabras que había dicho,
que a pesar de vos, señor,
se acostaría conmigo.'   20
Ya se arma Lanzarote
de gran pesar conmovido,
despídese de su amiga,
pregunta por el camino;
topó con el orgulloso   25
debajo de un verde pino,
combátense de las lanzas,
a las hachas han venido;
desmaya el orgulloso,
ya cae en tierra tendido,   30
cortárale la cabeza
sin hacer ningún partido;
vuélvese para su amiga
donde fue bien recibido.

TEXT: *Prim.* No. 148, from *Canc. de Rom.* *'sin año'* (c. 1548).

TRANSLATION: Gibson p. 385.

REFERENCE: *Tratado* II, 468, 473.

NOTES: Although the Spanish tales of Arthur and the Round Table, Merlin, Lancelot, etc., together with those of Tristram and Isolde, were occasionally printed in the first half of the 16th century, they were always at the time overshadowed in popularity by the rich native inventions of *Amadís* and company. Menéndez y Pelayo observes that although the Arthurian and Breton legends did not apparently have a place in Don Quixote's library, the Knight was well acquainted with them. He gave a brief lecture on the subject (I, 13), quoted the first four lines of this ballad and called it 'aquel tan sabido romance y tan decantado en nuestra España', and referred to it on other occasions.

58

Tres hijuelos había el rey,
tres hijuelos, que no más;
por enojo que hubo de ellos
todos maldito los ha:
el uno se tornó ciervo,   5
el otro se tornó can,
el otro se tornó moro,
pasó las aguas del mar.
Andábase Lanzarote
entre las damas holgando;   10
grandes voces dio la una:
'¡Caballero, estad parado!
Si fuese la mi ventura
cumplido fuese mi hado
que yo casase con vos   15
y vos conmigo de grado,
y me diésedes en arras
aquel ciervo del pie blanco.'
'Dároslo he yo, mi señora,
de corazón y de grado,   20
y supiese yo las tierras
donde el ciervo era criado.'
Ya cabalga Lanzarote,
ya cabalga y va su vía;
delante de sí llevaba   25
los sabuesos por la traílla.
Llegado había a una ermita
donde un ermitaño había:
'Dios te salve, el hombre bueno.'
'Buena sea tu venida;   30

114

cazador me parecéis
en los sabuesos que traía.'
'Dígasme tú, el ermitaño,
tú que haces santa vida,
ese ciervo del pie blanco   35
¿dónde hace su manida?'
'Quedáis os aquí, mi hijo,
hasta que sea de día;
contaros he lo que vi
y todo lo que sabía.   40
Por aquí pasó esta noche
dos horas antes del día,
siete leones con él
y una leona parida;
siete condes deja muertos   45
y mucha caballería.
Siempre Dios te guarde, hijo,
por doquier que fuer tu ida,
que quien acá te envió
no te quería dar la vida.   50
¡Ay dueña de Quintañones
de mal fuego seas ardida,
que tanto buen caballero
por ti ha perdido la vida!'

TEXT: *Prim.* No. 147, from *Canc. de Rom.* of 1550.

TRANSLATIONS: Gibson p. 387; Wright No. 13.

REFERENCES: *Tratado* II, 473-6; W.J. Entwistle, 'The Adventure of *Le Cerf au pied blanc* in Spanish and elsewhere', *Modern Language Review* 18 (1925) 435-48; Wright, *CG*, 74-5.

NOTES: The special charm of this ballad is its very strangeness. According to Entwistle it is very ancient (14th century), having been based on a Spanish prose tale of Lancelot but since 'cut down from a larger narrative to the point of obscurity'. Nebrija in his *Gramática castellana* of 1492 twice quotes lines of the ballad, in different versions, and calls it 'antiguo' by his time.

59

Yo me era mora Moraima,
morilla de un bel catar;
cristiano vino a mi puerta,
cuitada, por me engañar;
hablóme en algarabía   5

como aquél que la bien sabe:
'¡Abrasme las puertas, mora,
se Alá te guarde de mal!'
'¿Cómo te abriré, mezquina,
que no sé quién te serás?'   10
'Yo soy el moro Mazote,
hermano de la tu madre;
que un cristiano dejo muerto,
tras mí venía el alcalde;
si no me abres tú, mi vida,   15
aquí me verás matar.'
Cuando esto oí, cuitada,
comencéme a levantar;
vistiérame una almejía
no hallando mi brial,   20
fuérame para la puerta
y abríla de par en par.

TEXT: *Prim.* No. 132, from *Canc. de Rom. 'sin año'* (c. 1548).

TRANSLATION: Wright No. 66.

REFERENCES: *Tratado* II, 498; *Rom. hisp.* II, 11, 44-5; J.M. Sola-Solé, 'En torno al romance de la morilla burlada', *Hispanic Review* 33 (1965) 136-46; J.M. Aguirre, 'Moraima y el prisionero: ensayo de interpretación', in N.D. Shergold (ed.), *Studies of the Spanish and Portuguese Ballad* (London: Tamesis, 1972), 53-72; L. Mirrer-Singer, 'Reevaluating the *fronterizo* Ballad: The *Romance de la morilla burlada* as a pro-Christian Text', *La Corónica* 13 (1984-5) 157-67; Wright, *CG*, 75-8.

NOTES: This ballad is first known in a 32-line version contained in the *Cancionero de Londres* (compiled between 1471 and 1500). The present 22-line version is attributed in the *Cancionero general* of 1511 to Jerónimo de Pinar, and is so manifestly superior that it was the text printed in *pliegos sueltos* and then became the standard one. The extra ten lines have threats made by the Christian against the girl, and Pinar's instinct in removing them was sound. The ballad may certainly be termed 'morisco', but it is neither about war as the 15th-century *fronterizo* ballads are, nor sentimental and self-consciously exotic as are the true *morisco* ballads of the late 16th century; we have, rather, a small scene from the life of any southern Spanish town, turned into poetry by the charm of its opening lines and the enigma of its ending.

60

Yo me adamé una amiga
dentro en mi corazón;
Catalina había por nombre,
no la puedo olvidar, no.
Rogóme que la llevase 5
a las tierras de Aragón:
'Catalina, sois muchacha,
no podréis caminar, no.'
'Tanto andaré, el caballero,
tanto andaré como vos; 10
si lo dejáis por dineros
llevaré para los dos,
ducados para Castilla,
florines para Aragón.'
Ellos en aquesto estando 15
la justicia que llegó.

TEXT: *Prim.* No. 141, from *Canc. de Rom. 'sin año'* (c. 1548).

REFERENCE: *Rom. hisp.* I, 73.

NOTES: That this ballad has been abbreviated to the point of obscurity (so far as its theme is concerned) is a matter for pleasure rather than regret. It can be a tale of elopement, of a pair of *pícaros* on the run, or – best of all? – of a childish prank, as we wish. No more complete version exists to disturb our musings, although Menéndez Pidal was able to add 4 lines that were known to Gonzalo Correas in his *Vocabulario de refranes y frases proverbiales* of about 1630:

'Catalina, Catalina,
mucho me cuesta el tu amore,
tras mí viene la justicia,
también el corregidore.'

61

Fontefrida, Fontefrida,
Fontefrida y con amor,
do todas las avecicas
van tomar consolación,
si no es la tortolica 5
que está viuda y con dolor.
Por allí fuera a pasar
el traidor del ruiseñor;

117

las palabras que le dice
llenas son de traición: 10
'Si tú quisieses, señora,
yo sería tu servidor.'
'¡Vete de ahí, enemigo,
malo, falso, engañador!
Que ni poso en ramo verde 15
ni en prado que tenga flor,
que si el agua hallo clara
turbia la bebía yo;
que no quiero haber marido
porque hijos no haya, no; 20
no quiero placer con ellos,
ni menos consolación.
¡Déjame, triste, enemigo,
malo, falso, mal traidor,
que no quiero ser tu amiga 25
ni casar contigo, no!'

TEXT: *Prim.* No. 116, from *Cancionero de Constantina* and *Canc. de Rom.* *'sin año'* (c. 1548).

TRANSLATIONS: Gibson p. 372; Wright No. 8.

REFERENCES: *Tratado* II, 530-1; M. Bataillon, 'La tortolica de *Fonte-frida* y del *Cántico espiritual'*, *Nueva Revista de Filología Hispánica* 7 (1953) 291-306, reprinted in his book *Varia lección de clásicos españoles* (Madrid: Gredos, 1964), 144-66; E. Asensio, '*Fontefrida* o encuentro del romance con la canción de mayo', *Nueva Revista de Filología Hispánica*, 8 (1954) 365-88, reprinted in *Poesía y realidad en el cancionero peninsular de la Edad Media* 2nd ed. (Madrid: Gredos, 1970), 241-77; L. Calvert, 'Widowed Turtledove and Amorous Dove of Spanish Lyric poetry: A Symbolic Interpretation', *Journal of Medieval and Renaissance Studies* 3 (1973) 273-301; Wright, *CG*, 78-82.

NOTES: This ballad is a curious (and successful) mixture of a number of elements, some of great antiquity. It has the form of a *pastorela* or *serranilla* (dialogue between knight and shepherdess), and in its passionate tone is more lyrical than is customary in the ballads. The symbolism of dove, nightingale, fountain, etc., derives in part from learned written sources and in part from folklore. Gil Vicente seems to have adapted lines from the ballad for Cassandra's song in the *Auto da sibila Cassandra*: 'Dicen que me case yo;/no quiero marido, no.'

62

puede ser un hickname y love or her Real name "Rosa"

'Rosa fresca, Rosa fresca,
tan garrida y con amor,
cuando vos tuve en mis brazos
no vos supe servir, no;   }
y agora que os serviría   }   5
no vos puedo haber, no.'   }

→'Vuestra fue la culpa, amigo,
vuestra fue, que mía no:
enviástesme una carta
con un vuestro servidor,   10
y en lugar de recaudar
él dijera otra razón,
que érades casado, amigo,
allá en tierras de León,
que tenéis mujer hermosa   15
e hijos como una flor.'
'Quien os lo dijo, señora,
no vos dijo verdad, no;
que yo nunca entré en Castilla
ni allá en tierras de León   20
sino cuando era pequeño,
que no sabía de amor.'

TEXT: *Prim.* No. 115, from *Cancionero general* (1527 ed.) and *Canc. de Rom.'sin año'* (c. 1548).

TRANSLATIONS: Gibson p. 371; Wright No. 14.

REFERENCES: *Tratado* II, 503; *Rom. hisp.* II, 46-7; Wright, *CG*, 82.

NOTES: This seems to be one of the many ballads which has been cut down from a longer narrative to the point at which only the one essential scene is left. Its universal situation is still regularly (if less poetically) reflected on the 'problem page' of magazines. The ballad was popular at the court of the Catholic Monarchs about 1495, and throughout the Golden Age. Salinas, the blind organist of Salamanca, quotes lines of it and gives their tune in his book *De musica* of 1577. The first four lines are, according to Menéndez Pidal, still remembered in popular tradition.

63

A caza iban, a caza
los cazadores del rey;
ni fallaban ellos caza

ni fallaban qué traer;
perdido habían los halcones,   5
¡mal los amenaza el rey!
Arrimáranse a un castillo
que se llamaba Maynés;
dentro estaba una doncella
muy fermosa y muy cortés;   10
siete condes la demandan
y así facían tres reyes.
Robárala Rico Franco,
Rico Franco aragonés;
llorando iba la doncella   15
de sus ojos tan cortés;
halágala Rico Franco,
Rico Franco aragonés:
'Si lloras tu padre o madre
nunca más vos los veréis,   20
si lloras los tus hermanos
yo los maté todos tres.'
'No lloro padre ni madre,
ni hermanos todos tres;
mas lloro la mi ventura   25
que no sé cuál ha de ser.
Prestédesme, Rico Franco,
vuestro cuchillo lugués,
cortaré fitas al manto
que no son para traer.'   30
Rico Franco de cortese
por las cachas lo fue tender;
la doncella que era artera
por los pechos se lo fue a meter;
así vengó padre y madre   35
y aun hermanos todos tres.

TEXT: *Prim.* No. 119, from *Canc. de Rom. 'sin año'* (c. 1548).

TRANSLATION: Wright No. 4.

REFERENCES: *Tratado* II, 507-9; *Rom. hisp.* I, 330, and II, 316; Wright, *CG*, 83-4.

NOTES: This seems to be one of the most ancient and widely extended of all ballads, since forms of it are known in most European languages. Menéndez Pidal thinks it was brought into Spain from France, probably though Catalonia, and that in view of certain archaic forms it was printed

in the 1548 collection from a medieval manuscript. The ballad continues
to be widely known in Spain and among the Sephardim. Le Strange notes
that the 'cuchillo lugués' was one of the famous 'coltelli lucchesi' from
Lucca in Tuscany. The ballad seems to have suffered contamination with
Rosaflorida (No. 48).

64

'Blanca sois, señora mía,
más que el rayo del sol;
¿si la dormiré esta noche
desarmado y sin pavor?
Que siete años había, siete,   5
que no me desarmo, no;
más negras tengo mis carnes
que un tiznado carbón.'
'Dormidla, señor, dormidla
desarmado, sin temor,   10
que el conde es ido a caza
a los montes de León.'
'¡Rabia le mate los perros
y águilas el su halcón,
y del monte hasta casa   15
a él arrastre el morón!'
Ellos en aquesto estando
su marido que llegó:
'¿Qué hacéis, la Blancaniña,
hija de padre traidor?'   20
'Señor, peino mis cabellos,
péinolos con gran dolor,
que me dejáis a mí sola
y a los montes os vais vos.'
'Esa palabra, la niña,   25
no era sino traición:
¿cúyo es aquel caballo
que allá abajo relinchó?'
'Señor, era de mi padre,
y envióoslo para vos.'   30
'¿Cúyas son aquellas armas
que están en el corredor?'
'Señor, eran de mi hermano,
y hoy os las envió.'
'¿Cúya es aquella lanza,   35
desde aquí la veo yo?'

'¡Tomadla, conde, tomadla,
matadme con ella vos,
que aquesta muerte, buen conde,
bien os la merezco yo!'   40

TEXT: *Prim.* No. 136, from *Canc. de Rom.* of 1550.

TRANSLATION: Wright No. 1.

REFERENCES: *Tratado* II, 501; W.J. Entwistle, '*Blancaniña*', *Revista de Filología Hispánica* 1 (1939) 159-64; *Rom. hisp.* I, 332, and II, 176-7; Wright, *CG*, 84-8; Teresa Catarella, 'Feminine Historicizing in the *romancero novelesco*', *Bulletin of Hispanic Studies* 67 (1990) 331-43 (with full bibliography of modern oral versions).

NOTES: This and the next ballad are examples of a type known throughout Europe, on the theme 'the husband's return' (*La vuelta del marido*) or 'the punishment of the adulteress'. Versions closely or vaguely resembling our text are known throughout the Hispanic world, with endings which range from the tragic through the unstated to the comic, but in older times at least in Castile – country of Calderón and the *drama de honor* – the theme is treated with high seriousness. From the wonderfully sensual opening to the abrupt ending, this is a fine example of ballad technique. The poem has retained its popularity to the present day, and Menéndez Pidal remarks that 'A pesar de su asunto tan poco infantil, es de los más cantados por las niñas en el corro.' It was also recorded earlier this century, in a much-altered version, from the Jewish community of Tangiers. Teresa Catarella's study (1990) is a highly original feminist analysis of the very diverse attitudes and judgements implied in these poems.

65

'La bella malmaridada
de las lindas que yo vi,
véote tan triste, enojada,
la verdad díla tú a mí.
Si has de tomar amores   5
por otro no dejes a mí,
que a tu marido, señora,
con otras dueñas lo vi
besando y retozando;
mucho mal dice de ti,   10
juraba y perjuraba
que te había de ferir.'
    Allí habló la señora,
allí habló, y dijo así:

'Sácame tú, el caballero,   15
tú sacásesme de aquí;
por las tierras donde fueres
bien te sabría yo servir;
yo te haría bien la cama
en que hayamos de dormir,   20
yo te guisaré la cena
como a caballero gentil,
de gallinas y de capones
y otras cosas más de mil;
que a este mi marido   25
ya no le puedo sufrir,
que me da muy mala vida
cual vos bien podéis oir.'
   Ellos en aquesto estando
su marido hélo aquí: 30
'¿Qué hacéis, mala traidora?
¡Hoy habedes de morir!'
'¿Y por qué, señor, por qué?
que nunca os lo merecí;
nunca besé a hombre,   35
mas hombre besó a mí;
las penas que él merecía
señor, dadlas vos a mí;
con riendas de tu caballo
señor, azotes a mí;   40
con cordones de oro y sirgo
viva ahorques a mí;
en la huerta de los naranjos
viva entierres tú a mí,
en sepultura de oro   45
y labrada de marfil,
y pongas encima un mote,
señor, que diga así:
"Aquí está la flor de las flores,
por amores murió aquí;   50
cualquier que muere de amores
mándese enterrar aquí,
que así hice yo, mezquina,
que por amar me perdí".'

TEXT: *Prim.* No. 142, from a *pliego suelto* of the 16th century.

TRANSLATIONS: Lockhart No. 55, 'The Ill-married Lady'; Wright No. 2.

REFERENCES: *Tratado* II, 503-6; D. Lucero de Padrón, 'En torno al romance de *La bella malmaridada*', *Boletín de la Biblioteca Menéndez Pelayo* 43 (1967) 307-54; Wright, *CG*, 88-9.

NOTES: This ballad was probably composed in the late 15th century, and achieved great popularity in the 16th with musicians and *glosadores*. The moralising ending was added in an edition of 1551, according to Menéndez Pidal.

66

Estáse la gentil dama
paseando en su vergel,
los pies tenía descalzos
que era maravilla ver;
desde lejos me llamara,   5
no le quise responder;
respondíle con gran saña:
'¿Qué mandáis, gentil mujer?'
Con una voz amorosa
comenzó de responder: 10
'Ven acá, el pastorcico,
si quieres tomar placer;
siesta es de mediodía
que ya es hora de comer,
si querrás tomar posada   15
todo es a tu placer.'
    'Que no era tiempo, señora,
que me haya de detener;
que tengo mujer e hijos
y casa de mantener,   20
y mi ganado en la sierra
que se me iba a perder,
y aquéllos que me lo guardan
no tenían que comer.'
'Vete con Dios, pastorcillo,   25
no te sabes entender,
hermosuras de mi cuerpo
yo te las hiciera ver;
delgadica en la cintura,
blanca soy como el papel,   30
la color tengo mezclada
como rosa en el rosel,
el cuello tengo de garza

124

los ojos de un esparver,
la teticas agudicas   35
que el brial quieren romper;
pues lo que tengo encubierto
maravilla es de lo ver.'
'Ni aunque más tengáis, señora,
no me puedo detener.'   40

TEXT: *Prim.* No. 145, from a *pliego suelto* of the 16th century.

TRANSLATION: Wright No.. 12.

REFERENCES: *Tratado* II, 524-6; E. Levi, 'El romance florentino de Jaume de Olesa', *Revista de Filología Española* 14 (1927) 134-60; L. Spitzer, 'Observaciones sobre el romance florentino de Jaume de Olesa', *ibid.* 22 (1935) 153-8; *Rom. hisp.* I, 339-44; *Rom. trad.*, X-XI; Wright, *CG*, 88-9.

NOTES: A version or ancestor of this poem is the earliest known written text of a Spanish ballad, set down in a notebook in 1421 by the Majorcan student Jaume de Olesa when at an Italian university. It begins, in mixed Castilian-Catalan:

Gentil dona, gentil dona,
dona de bell paresser,
los pes tingo en la verdura
esperando este plaser.
Por hi passa ll'escudero
mesurado e cortés;
las paraules que me dixo
todes eren d'emorés:
'Tate, escudero, este coerpo,
este corpo a tu plaser...'

This was far from new even in Olesa's day, according to Menéndez Pidal; an 'escudero' has already replaced the original 'pastorcico' (who is, however, preserved in our *pliego suelto* version). The poem is basically a sort of *pastorela* or *serranilla* in reverse, though without the mocking exaggerations which Juan Ruiz put into his burlesque *serranillas* in the 14th century. The poem may ultimately have originated in France. Derivations of the ballad, in a variety of non-ballad forms, are known to have been popular throughout the Golden Age, and these survive in our times in many parts of Spain and among the Spanish Jews, mostly in versions with strongly moralised endings.

67

A cazar va el caballero,
a cazar como solía,
los perros lleva cansados,
el halcón perdido había,
arrimárase a un roble   5
alto es a maravilla;
en una rama más alta
viera estar una infantina,
cabellos de su cabeza
todo el roble cubrían: 10
'No te espantes, caballero,
ni tengas tamaña grima;
hija soy yo del buen rey
y de la reina de Castilla;
siete fadas me fadaron   15
en brazos de una ama mía,
que andase los siete años
sola en esta montiña.
Hoy se cumplían los siete años
o mañana en aquel día.   20
Por Dios te ruego, caballero,
llévesme en tu compañía,
si quisieres por mujer,
si no, sea por amiga.'
'Esperéisme vos, señora,   25
hasta mañana, aquel día,
iré yo a tomar consejo
de una madre que tenía.'
La niña le respondiera
y estas palabras decía: 30
'¡Oh mal haya el caballero
que sola deja la niña!'
El se va a tomar consejo,
y ella queda en la montiña.
Aconsejóle su madre   35
que la tomase por amiga.
Cuando volvió el caballero
no la hallara en la montiña;
vídola que la llevaban
con muy gran caballería.   40
El caballero desque la vido

126

en el suelo se caía;
desque en sí hubo tornado
estas palabras decía:
'Caballero que tal pierde   45
muy gran pena merecía;
yo mismo seré el alcalde,
yo me seré la justicia:
que le corten pies y manos
y lo arrastren por la villa.'   50

TEXT: *Prim.* No. 151, from *Canc. de Rom. 'sin año'* (c. 1548).

TRANSLATIONS: Lockhart No. 29, 'The Lady of the Tree'; Gibson p. 369;
Wright No. 19.

REFERENCES: *Tratado* II, 519-21; D. Devoto, 'El mal cazador', in *Studia
Philologica: Homenaje ofrecido a Dámaso Alonso* (Madrid: Gredos,
1960), I, 481-91; Wright, *CG*, 89-90.

NOTES: The fairy-tale theme of this ballad is unusual in the context of the
Romancero but is found throughout Europe. Menéndez y Pelayo suggests
it may have originated in Celtic folklore. The ballad does not seem to be
well known in the oral tradition, but versions have been recorded from the
Canaries and Venezuela.

68

'Vengo brindado, Mariana,
para una boda el domingo.'
'Esa boda, don Alonso,
debiera de ser conmigo.'
'No es conmigo, Mariana;   5
es con un hermano mío.'
'Siéntate aquí, don Alonso,
en este escaño florido,
que me lo dejó mi padre
para el que case conmigo.'   10
Se sentara don Alonso,
presto se quedó dormido;
Mariana como discreta
se fue a su jardín florido;
tres onzas de solimán,   15
cuatro de acero molido,
la sangre de tres culebras,
la piel de un lagarto vivo,
y la espinilla del sapo

127

todo se lo echó en el vino.   20
  'Bebe vino, don Alonso,
don Alonso, bebe vino.'
'Bebe primero, Mariana,
que así está puesto en estilo.'
Mariana como discreta   25
por el pecho lo ha vertido;
don Alonso como joven
todo el vino se ha bebido;
con la fuerza del veneno
los dientes se le han caído.   30
  '¿Qué es esto, Mariana?
¿Qué es esto que tiene el vino?'
'Tres onzas de solimán,
cuatro de acero molido,
la sangre de tres culebras   35
la piel de un lagarto vivo,
y la espinilla del sapo
para robarte el sentido.'
  '¡Sáname, buena Mariana,   *If you cure me, I'll marry you*
que me casaré contigo!'   40
  'No puede ser, don Alonso,   *she says she can't, his ♡ is alredy*
que el corazón te ha partido.'   *dying.*
  '¡Adiós, esposa del alma,
presto quedas sin marido!
¡Adiós, padres de mi vida,   45
presto quedaron sin hijo!
Cuando salí de mi casa
salí en un caballo pío,
y ahora voy para la iglesia
en una caja de pino.'   50

TEXT: Recorded in Asturias in the 1870s by Juan Menéndez Pidal, and printed by Menéndez y Pelayo among the *Romances populares*, vol. X of the *Antología de poetas líricos*, p. 98.

TRANSLATION: Wright No. 7.

REFERENCES: *Tratado* II, 509-12; Wright, *CG*, 90-1.

NOTES: Versions of this ballad are known from various Spanish provinces, and in Portuguese from the Azores and Brazil. In a Catalan version the girl is called 'Gudriana', a name which leads Menéndez y Pelayo to suppose that the theme may have a Germanic origin. This is an example of a ballad known only from the oral tradition, although it is certainly ancient.

69

'Que por mayo era, por mayo,
cuando hace la calor,
cuando los trigos encañan
y están los campos en flor,
cuando canta la calandria   5
y responde el ruiseñor,
cuando los enamorados
van a servir al amor;
sino yo, triste, cuitado,
que vivo en esta prisión,   10
que no sé cuando es de día
ni cuando las noches son,
sino por una avecilla
que me cantaba al albor.
Matómela un ballestero,   15
¡déle Dios mal galardón!'

[handwritten note: describe the month / of may: temp, naturaleza / estación de / primavera]

TEXT: In part *Prim.* Nos. 114 and 114a, based on the *Cancionero general* version of 1511, with the addition of two lines (3 & 4) from the version given by Menéndez Pidal in *Flor nueva de romances viejos*.

TRANSLATIONS: Lockhart No. 54, 'The Captive Knight and the Blackbird'; Gibson p. 367; Wright, two versions, Nos. 5 (1) & 5 (2).

REFERENCES: *Tratado* II, 528; *Rom. hisp.*, II, 45; Wright, *CG*, 91-3; D. Devoto, 'Calandrias y ruiseñores (sobre los versos siempre nuevos de los romances viejos', *Bulletin Hispanique* 92 (1990) 259-307; D. McGrady, 'Misterio y tradición en el romance del Prisionero', in *Actas del X Congreso de la Asociación Internacional de Hispanistas* [Barcelona, August 1989] (Barcelona: PPU, 1992), 273-82 (with full bibliography).

NOTES: This ballad is famous for the intense lyricism of the prisoner's lament, the more painful for being so brief and plain. Its balance, alliterations, and subtleties of rhythm are most delicately contrived, as is the sequence of images – each more warm and physical than the last – by which the prisoner realises the total tragedy of his situation. Some of these qualities are present in the longer version given by the *Cancionero de romances* of 1550, but the poem's universality, its lyricism untainted by a single narrative note, and the unresolved ending, are stronger features of the short text. The longer version of 1550 has 40 lines; it continues beyond our text to give details of the prisoner's condition, the name of his wife, and the hope that she can smuggle in to him a file with which he might saw through his bars. This version then has a happy ending:

Oídolo había el rey,
mandóle quitar la prisión.

In this state the ballad is nothing very special. Most critics and editors have assumed that (as in other cases) the longer narrative version is the original and that the masterly short version is the result of judicious truncation. But McGrady (1992) holds that the 'extra' lines are a grossly inferior addition which destroys the tensions of the short text, and once this is cogently argued, it is readily possible to agree with him. McGrady has further notes on the antiquity of the 'bird-as-lovers'-messenger' theme. In its various forms the ballad seems to have been well known throughout the Golden Age, and its opening lines were often quoted. It has been found by modern collectors in the provinces of Burgos and Santander as a part of the spring festivities known as *marzas*, and in many other parts of Spain and Spanish America.

The ballad has curious echoes from beyond the Pyrenees. In the French epic *Amis et Amiles* (which we can be sure from other evidence was known in Spain) we find 'Ce fu en may que chante la calandre' (line 513), and in the Occitan *Ronsasvals* 'El temps que fon la Santa Cros passeya/Ans Pandecosta, cant canta la copeya' (lines 181-2). This might have been a commonplace among Occitan troubadours and singers, many of whom are recorded at Spanish royal and noble courts in the 12th and 13th centuries.

70

¡Quién hubiese tal ventura
sobre las aguas del mar
como hubo el conde Arnaldos
la mañana de San Juan!
Con un halcón en la mano   5
la caza iba a cazar,
vio venir una galera
que a tierra quiere llegar.
Las velas traía de seda,
la ejercia de un cendal;   10
marinero que la manda
diciendo viene un cantar
que la mar hacía en calma,
los vientos hace amainar,
los peces que andan al hondo   15
arriba los hace andar,
las aves que andan volando
en el mástil las hace posar.
Allí habló el conde Arnaldos,

bien oiréis lo que dirá: 20
'Por Dios te ruego, marinero,
dígasme ora ese cantar.'
Respondióle el marinero,
tal respuesta le fue a dar:
'Yo no digo esta canción 25
sino a quien conmigo va.'

TEXT: *Prim.* No. 153, from *Canc. de Rom. 'sin año'* (c. 1548).

TRANSLATIONS: Lockhart No. 46, 'Count Arnaldos'; Gibson p. 390; Wright No. 20 (variant version). The merits of no fewer than nine English versions are assessed by F. Caravaca in *La Torre* (Puerto Rico) 18-19 (1970-1) 221-71, among them the free but very successful rendering by Longfellow, 'The Secret of the Sea', published in *The Seaside and the Fireside* in 1850:

> Ah! what pleasant visions haunt me
> As I gaze upon the sea!
> All the old romantic legends,
> All my dreams, come back to me.
>   Sails of silk and ropes of sandal
> Such as gleam in ancient lore;
> And the singing of the sailors,
> And the answer from the shore!...

REFERENCES: *Tratado* II, 531-3; *Rom. hisp.* I, 74, etc.; R. Menéndez Pidal, *Poesía popular y poesía tradicional* (Oxford: OUP, 1922), 9-19; L. Spitzer, 'Notas sobre romances españoles', *Revista de Filología Española* 22 (1935) 158-61; L. Spitzer, 'The Folkloristic Pre-stage of the Spanish *romance* "Count Arnaldos" ', *Hispanic Review* 23 (1955) 173-87, with addenda *ibid.*, 24 (1956) 64-6, both articles being reprinted in *Sobre antigua poesía española* (Buenos Aires: Universidad de Buenos Aires, 1962), 87-103; various studies by F. Caravaca, mentioned in the latest, 'Tres nuevas aportaciones al estudio del *Romance del Conde Arnaldos*', *Boletín de la Biblioteca Menéndez Pelayo* 49 (1973) 183-228; M. Débax, 'Yo no digo esta canción/sino a quien conmigo va', in *Mélanges offerts à M. Molho* (Paris: Éditions Hispaniques, 1988), I, 55-68; Wright, *CG*, 93-5.

NOTES: No ballad has commanded such universal admiration and interest as this. It is a thing perfect of its kind, catching the movement of the sea in its various moods by subtle changes of rhythm, and expressing something of the mystery of the sea not only in its description of the magic galley and the sailor's song but also in its ending. This ending is, as in other cases, no accident, but the result of judicious truncation in the early 16th century. Other versions are known: a very confused and already contaminated one set down by Juan

Spanish Ballads

Rodríguez del Padrón in 1430-40, and others with a few additional lines printed in the 1550 and later editions of the *Cancionero de romances* and in a *pliego suelto*. The 'full' version was discovered comparatively recently among the Sephardic Jews. It completes the shorter text as follows:

> Tiró la barca el navío
> y el infante fue a embarcar;
> alzan velas, caen remos,
> comienzan a navegar.
> con el ruido del agua
> el sueño le venció ya.
> Pónenle los marineros
> los hierros de cautivar.
> A los golpes del martillo
> el infante fue a acordar:
> 'Por tu vida, el marinero,
> no me quieras hacer mal;
> hijo soy del rey de Francia,
> nieto dél de Portugal;
> siete años había, siete,
> que fui perdido en la mar.'
> Allí le habló el marinero:
> 'Si tú me dices verdad,
> tú eres nuestro infante Arnaldos
> y a ti andamos a buscar.'
> Alzó velas el navío
> y se van a la ciudad.
> Torneos y más torneos,
> que el conde pareció ya.

The relative merits of the two versions have been debated by Menéndez Pidal and Spitzer. No one doubts the appeal of the short text. The long text is called by Menéndez Pidal 'sin duda, un buen romance de aventura marítima, pero no alcanza la eficacia poética que tan notablemente distingue a la versión trunca'. Spitzer sees much more in the long text: not only the fine sea-rhythms of its third and fourth lines, which lull the Count to sleep, but folklore elements of some antiquity and complexity which make the whole poem a tale about the stealing away of mortals into fairyland. For this interpretation it is important to note that the pause between lines 8 and 9 of the long version, between the shackling of the Count and his awakening, is a pause of no less than seven years 'que fui perdido en la mar'. There is no doubt that the original poem reached Spain from France; 'Arnaldos' has the *-os* typical of French names in Spain, from *Arnaud*, *Arnault(s)*, in another form *Renaud*.

GLOSSARY

NOTE: The translation given in each case is not a complete one but is intended solely to give the meaning required by the ballad text. Numbers refer to those of the ballads.

abarca *f* sandal
abollar to dent
acerado with a steel tip
acicalar to polish
adamar to fall madly in love with
adarga *f* shield
adarve *m* sentry-walk (*on top of a wall*)
adelantado *m* governor of a frontier area
ado where
afamar to restore the good name of
afinar to polish
aguijada *f* slash with a spur
aguinaldo *m*: **en** – as a present
alarido *m* shout
alazán, alazano sorrel
albergar to take in, give lodging to
albornoz *m* Moorish cape, burnouse
alcaide *m* warder, jailer (7); governor of a castle (38)
alcalde *m* judge (59, 67)
alcandora *f* white tunic
¡alcarria! shame on you! (41: *the Moor is quoting the start of a chapter of the Koran, where* al-qari'a *means* 'the final retribution', *that is* 'the Day of Judgement'; *see* A.R. Nykl in *Modern Philology* 17 (1917) 167.
aleve *m* treachery
alevoso *m* traitor
alfanje *m* sword, scimitar
alfaquí *m* religious leader, teacher of the Koran
alférez *m* knight (*Arabic* al-faras 'horse') *or* queen (*Arabic* al-ferza 'queen', *in chess*); *see* A.R. Nykl in *Modern Philology* 17 (1917) 168
algarabía *f* Arabic
alguacil *m* man-at-arms, henchman (49, 54); constable (54)
alhaleme *m* veil
aliñado: mal – not very sensible
aljuba *f* Moorish cloak

almejía *f* Moorish cloak of rough cloth
almete *m* helmet
alnado *m* stepson
allegar (*intransitive*) to arrive; (*transitive*) to bring up
allén, allende beyond (44, 49); overseas, beyond the seas (1)
amainar to slacken, fall calm
amiga *f* mistress
añafil *m* Moorish pipe
andanza: de mala – wicked
aparejar to get ready, prepare
aparejo *m* aid
apellido *m* war-cry
aquejar to pain
aquese *etc.* that
aqueste *etc.* this
arboledo *m* bushy plant
ardid bold, brave
arma *f:* **tocar al –** to sound the call to arms
armar to set up (19 *etc.*); to load (*crossbow*: 34); to fit out (*ships*: 47); to
    bear, carry (*arms*: 25); to hold (*Cortes*: 24); to plan (*treachery*: 22)
arrabal *m* outlying suburb of a town
arráez *m* chief, captain
arrancada: lleváronnos de – they swept us before them
arras *fpl* property settled upon the bride as part of a marriage contract
arremeter to spur on (*horse*: 8); **– con** to close with (*in battle*: 27)
arrendar to rein back
asaz more than a little
asentar: – el campo to pitch camp
asomada *f:* **a la – de un llano** overlooking a plain
azagaya *f* spear

ballesta *f* crossbow
ballestero *m* crossbowman
baraja *f* dispute, brawl
baranda *f* railing
barragán *m* brave man
bascas *fpl* signs of disgust
bastida *f* mobile siege-tower
batalla *f* battle-line, front (2); squadron (35); army (39)
batel *m* boat
bayo bay, reddish-brown
bohordar: the game or exercise so called consisted of throwing heavy
    wooden darts at the *tablado* (*q.v.*) in an effort to knock it down

Glossary

bonete *m* cap
borceguí *m* half-boot, high shoe
bordón *m* pilgrim's staff
bracero *m* strong-armed man
brasa *f* live coal
bregas *fpl* strife
brial *m* tunic
brindar to invite
broslar to embroider

cabalgada *f* cavalry raid (32); troop of horsemen (28, 29, 31)
caballería *f* cavalry, horsemen (30, 58, *etc.*); group of horsemen (7, 22)
caballero: – en riding on
cabe near, close to
cachas *fpl* handle, haft
cachicuernos: cuchillo – knife with a horn handle
caja *f* (**de guerra**) drum
calandria *f* skylark
calzada *f* highroad
calzar *m* shoe
camarero *m* page-boy
camisón *m* smock
campal pitched (*battle*)
can *m* dog
caños *mpl* aqueduct
capellar *m* hat
carcañal *m* heelbone
carrillo *m* cheek
casa *f* **de Meca** mosque
catar to see; **de un bel –** good-looking; **por celos que dél cataba** because he was jealous of him
caza *f* rout (44)
cebada *f* barley, fodder
cebar to feed
cebra *f* wild ass, onager
celada *f* ambush
cendal *m* fine silk material, gauze
cerrojo *m* bolt
cibera *f* grain, corn (*for milling*)
cincha *f* horse's girth
colodrillo *m* back of the neck
colorado red
combatir to attack (27, 30)

compaña *f* company, army (5, 21); armed retinue (10)
conseja *f* tale
consejada *f* agreed plan
contray *m* a fine cloth
coraje *m*: **si me toman los –s** if anger takes control of me
cordel *m* rope
cordobán *m* Cordovan leather
correr to raid (32)
cortes *fpl* court, judicial assembly
cras tomorrow
cuadrillo *m* shaft, arrow
cuestión *f*: **mover una –** to start an argument
cuidar to think, imagine (1); to intend to (10)
cuita *f*: **con –** under stress
cuitado wretched
cumplido virtuous

dádiva *f* gift
daga *f* dagger
demanda *f* enterprise
demandar to ask (51, 54); to ask for (22); to ask for (*something*) back (21); to seek in marriage (48, 63); to make a complaint about (26); **te será bien demandada** you will be called to account for it (5); **demándelo su pecado** may the devil take his own! (26)
dende from
denodado bold, fearless
denunciar to announce
derribar to put aside, take off (8)
desmesurado violent (8)
desque as soon as
discrepar: si yo fuese en –lo if I were the cause of breaking it up
do where
doliente gravely ill
domeñar to rule; to conquer

ejercia *f* rigging
enamorada *f* mistress (21, 28, 46); **siete años ha...que soy vuestra –** I have been in love with you for seven years
encañar: cuando los trigos encañan when the wheat stalks begin to grow tall
encenagado: como puerca encenagada like a sow in the mire
enderezarse to stand up
enhorcar to hang

enjaezar: enjaezado de grana with scarlet trappings
escanciar to pour out (*wine*)
escaño *m* bench, ceremonial chair
esmaltar to adorn
esparver *m* sparrow-hawk
esposas *fpl* handcuffs
estancia *f* room

fementido treacherous
filo: por – exactly
finado *m* dead man
fincar to stay
fita *f* ribbon or tag for fastening cloaks *etc.*
florido red in the face, flushed
fogueado hardened by fire, hardened by boiling
frisado *m* silk plush

galardón *m* reward
galardonar to reward
garrido beautiful
gentil beautiful (66); noble (47, 65)
gesto *m* face (26); **su – muy demudado** his face contorted with anger
gracia *f*: **de –** free; **¿cómo era la tu –?** what is your name?
grima *f* fear, horror
guarir to cure (34); **– de** to recover from (*wounds*: 47)
guarnido rich, powerful

heredad *f* estate
hideperro *m* bastard
hideputa *m* bastard
hijasdalgo: dueñas – noblewomen
hijodalgo *m* nobleman
hito: mirar en – to stare (*someone*) up and down
holanda *f* fine linen. cambric
holgar to please, give pleasure to (44); to rest (54); to live in luxury (58);
    – con to make love to (7, 23, 25, 54, *etc.*); **–se con** to be pleased with;
    a bel – at their pleasure (54)
hueste *f* host, army

jara *f* thicket
jaral *m* scrub
jerga *f* coarse cloth
jineta: caballero a la – riding with high stirrups and bent legs

jornada *f* day (5); day's journey, stage (6, 23, 51); enterprise, attack (28)
jubón *m* doublet
jura *f* oath
juro: de – as of right, with full legal possession

labrar to build (33); to embroider (20, 30, 46); **labrada de marfil** worked
    in ivory (65)
lasamente wearily
librar: quedaba mejor librado came off best; **yo soy quien mejor**
    librara I was best able to get away
lid *f* battle
lombarda *f* lombard (*an ancient cannon*)
loriga *f* breastplate
lozanía *f* pride, haughtiness; **con** – arrogantly
lozano handsome, beautiful

maestro *m* surgeon
malo: si mala me la dijere if he should answer me no
mallado mailed, of mail
mancilla *f* pity (50, 54); **que de verle era** – the sight of him filled one with
    pity (3); **con** – **que dél han** out of the pity they feel for him (50); **gran**
    – **en sí tenía** he was filled with grief (3); – **es de la escuchar** it fills
    one with sorrow to hear of it; **con** – in dishonour (25)
mandar to promise (8)
manera: sobre – excessive, overwhelming
manida *f* haunts, lair
manjar *m* food
mantón *m* cloak
maña *f*: **malas –s** evil ways
marlota *f* Moorish gown
maravilla *f*: **a** – marvellously (2, 35); in the most terrible fashion (7)
mayoral *mf* overseer
menguado: en hora menguada in an unlucky hour
mensajería *f* message
mercedes *fpl* thanks
mesurado prudent
misa *f*: **misa rezada** low mass (*without music; in 56, the lovers' kiss lasts*
    as long as this mass)
mocho flat-topped (*tower*)
mojón *m* boundary-stone
monumento *m* bier
morcillo reddish-black (*horse*)

morería *f* Moorish quarter (15); Moors, Moorish population (30, 33);
Moorish religion (45)

morisma *f* Moors (*collectively*)

morón *m* dark brown or black horse

mote *m* inscription

mustio downcast

notar to check (1)

novena *f* novena (*special prayers on nine successive days*)

nuevas *fpl* news

palo: de – wooden

palomar *m* dovecote

pan *m* wheat (41)

par: en – del río down beside the river

pasa *f* raisin

patada *f* hoofbeat

pecho *m* tax (9)

pedrería *f*: **que eran de gran –** which were covered with precious stones

peón *m* foot-soldier

perlado *m* prelate, bishop

petral *m* breast-strap

pío piebald (*horse*)

pleitesía *f*: **a –** on terms

pleito *m* complaint (57)

podenca *f* hound

poder: con el – de la gente in the press of people

poderes *mpl* forces, troops

poridad *f* secrecy

portillo *m* breach

postigo *m* postern gate

postrimería *f* end, last days

pretal *m* breast strap

puerco espín *m* wild boar

puerto *m* pass (43)

quedo: de – quietly

querellarse to complain

querer + *inf.* to be about to (15, 49, 54, *etc.*); **que quería reventar** as
though he would burst (50, 54); **quiera...quiera** either...or (26)

quintal *m* hundredweight

Spanish Ballads

rastrillo *m* portcullis
real *m* royal camp, army headquarters
recaudar to guard, protect
recordar to wake up (49, 56)
repartidor: –en su haber generous with his wealth
retar to challenge
retornar: no la pueden – they cannot bring her round
retraer to reproach
revolver: –te hían guerra they would stir up war against you
rico: ricos hombres noblemen
rocín, rocino *m* hack, horse
romería *f* pilgrimage
romero *m* pilgrim
ropas *fpl*: – **continas** everyday clothes; – **de pascua** best clothes
roquete *m* barbed spear

saltear to raid
sandío: loca sandía raving mad
sayal *m* coarse woollen cloth
sayo *m* tunic, smock
señalado special
señoría *f* realm
siesta *f* heat (13)
siniestro left
sirgo *m* silk stuff
so under
sobarbada *f* reproach
soldada *f* pay
solimán *m* corrosive sublimate
soltar to explain (*dream*: 45)
sonada *f* boasting, boastful talk

tablado *m* structure of planks, mock castle, at which darts were thrown in
     the game or exercise of *bohordar* (10); table of planks (12)
tablas *fpl* checkers
tamaño so great, such
telilla *f*: – **les tengo urdida** I have woven such a web for them
tenencia *f* fief (6); rule (38)
tinto: – **de sangre** bloodstained
tiznado coal-black
toca *f* cap (30); **tocas** *fpl* head-dress (25)
tocar: toca llevaba tocada he had a cap on his head
tomar: todos de armas – all capable of bearing arms

tornabodas *fpl* second part of the wedding festivities (*at bridegroom's home*)
tornadizo *m* renegade (*Christian converted to Islam*)
tornido turned on a lathe
tranzado braided, plaited
traspasar to hand over
tullido maimed

ufano proud, noble

vagar: no de – with all possible speed
vara *f* dart, shaft
varica *f* staff
vellido fine, handsome
venablo *m* javelin
vergel *m* garden, orchard
viandas *fpl* food
villa *f* town
villano *m* villein
vira *f* dart

yantar *f* meal; (*verb*) to have lunch

zafira: piedra – sapphire
zarzahán *m* striped silk

INDEX OF FIRST LINE

Glossary

Current and forthcoming titles
in the BCP Spanish Texts Series: